My Jesus
Donna Freitag

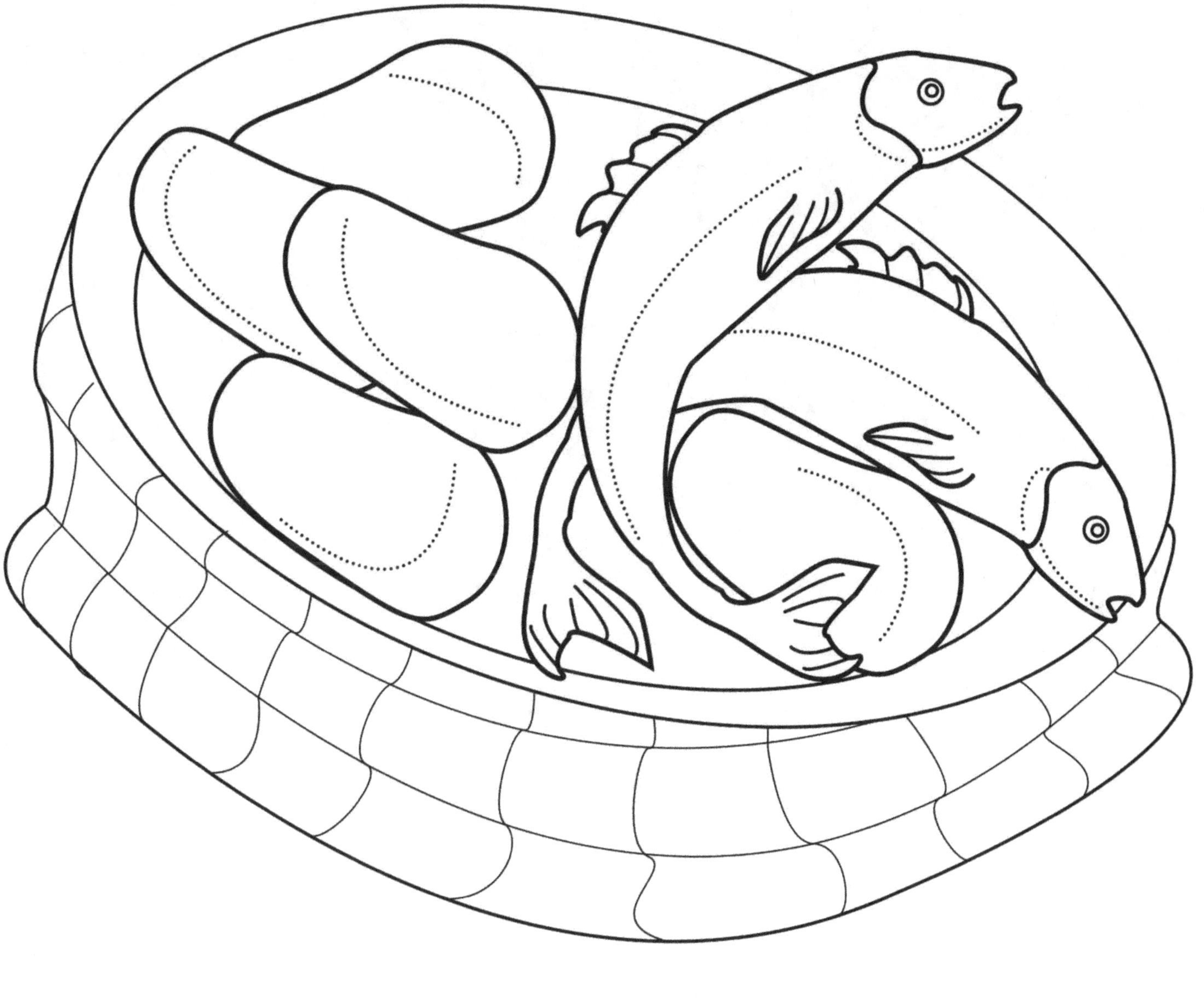

DonnaFreitag.com

How to color this book

My Jesus is a coloring book for adults. You'll enjoy hours of creative, relaxing, stress relieving fun as you color 25 all new space age designs. All are beautiful, new, original artwork never before seen in any collection.

Coloring Tips

Colored pencils are the most popular way to color. It's best to get a large set of at least 48 colors. Some of the best brands are Prismacolor and Staedtler.

In addition, you'll need an eraser and a good pencil sharpener. Also popular are markers. Warning: they tend to bleed through the page. So if you use them, place a sheet or thick paper underneath so the ink doesn't leak onto the picture below. Copic markers are a great brand.

Marker sets offer a smaller choice of colors than pencil sets. That's one reason why the pro colorists often use a combination of pencils, markers, gel pens and even crayons.

It all depends on the effects you want to produce.

Please post photos of your artwork on my Facebook page. I'd love to see what you've done!

Be sure to follow us on social media...

f donnafreitag90

t @donna_r_freitag

Ig @donnafreitag1991

P donna_freitag

Join our mailing list for the latest news and freebies.

Visit www.donnafreitag.com

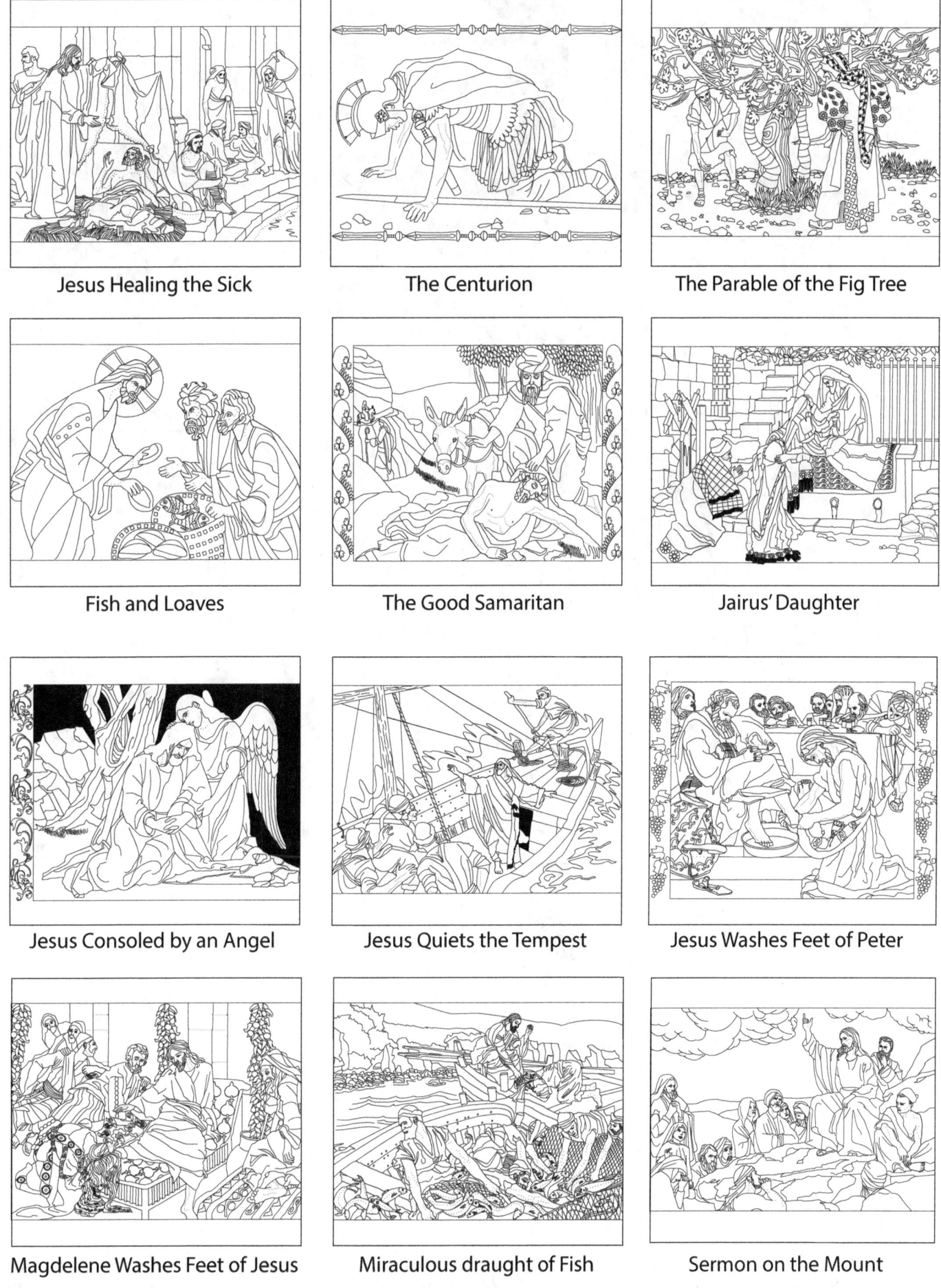

Jesus Healing the Sick

The Centurion

The Parable of the Fig Tree

Fish and Loaves

The Good Samaritan

Jairus' Daughter

Jesus Consoled by an Angel

Jesus Quiets the Tempest

Jesus Washes Feet of Peter

Magdelene Washes Feet of Jesus

Miraculous draught of Fish

Sermon on the Mount

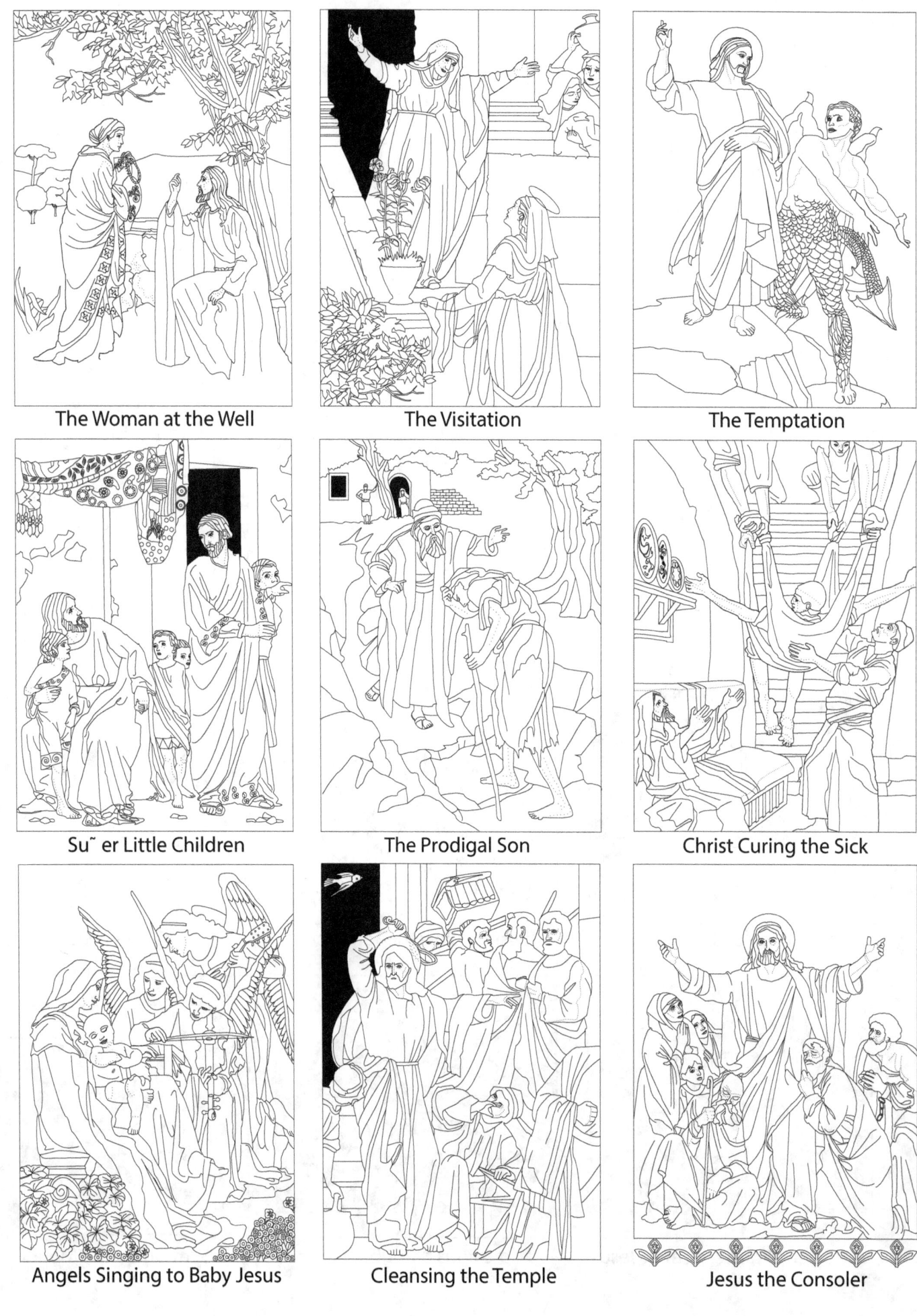

The Woman at the Well

The Visitation

The Temptation

Su˜er Little Children

The Prodigal Son

Christ Curing the Sick

Angels Singing to Baby Jesus

Cleansing the Temple

Jesus the Consoler

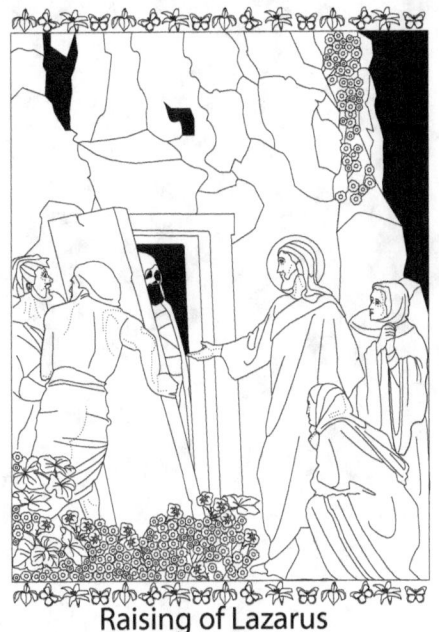

Raising of Lazarus

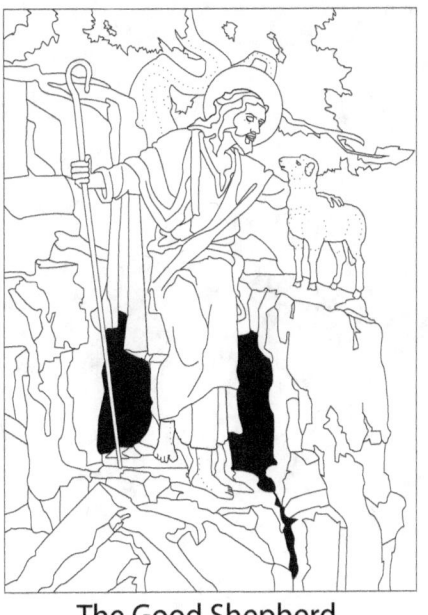

The Good Shepherd

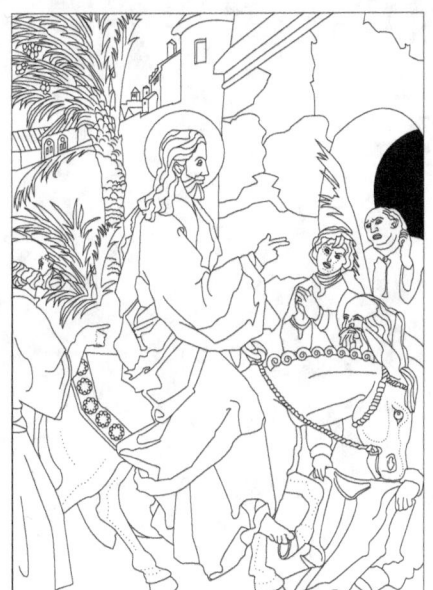

Palm Sunday

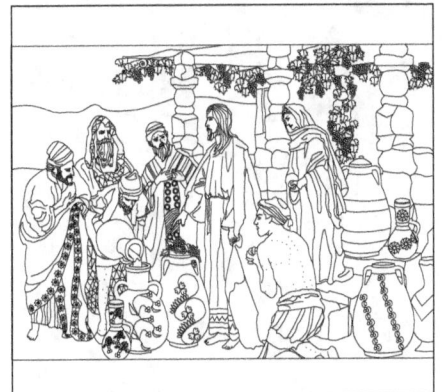

The Wedding at Cana

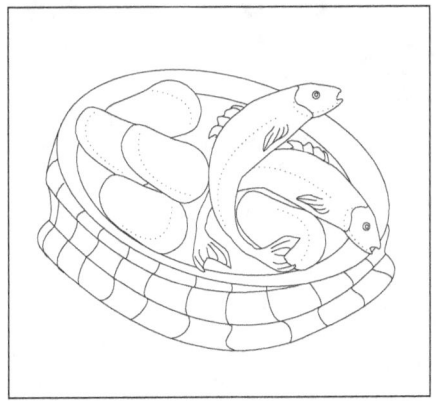

Two Fish, Five Loaves

Download FREE
PDF Images for even
more coloring fun at
Donnafreitag.com
Click on Freebies

"And it came to pass, that when Elizabeth
heard the salutation of Mary,
the infant leaped in her womb.
And Elizabeth was filled with the Holy Ghost:"
[Luke 1:41]

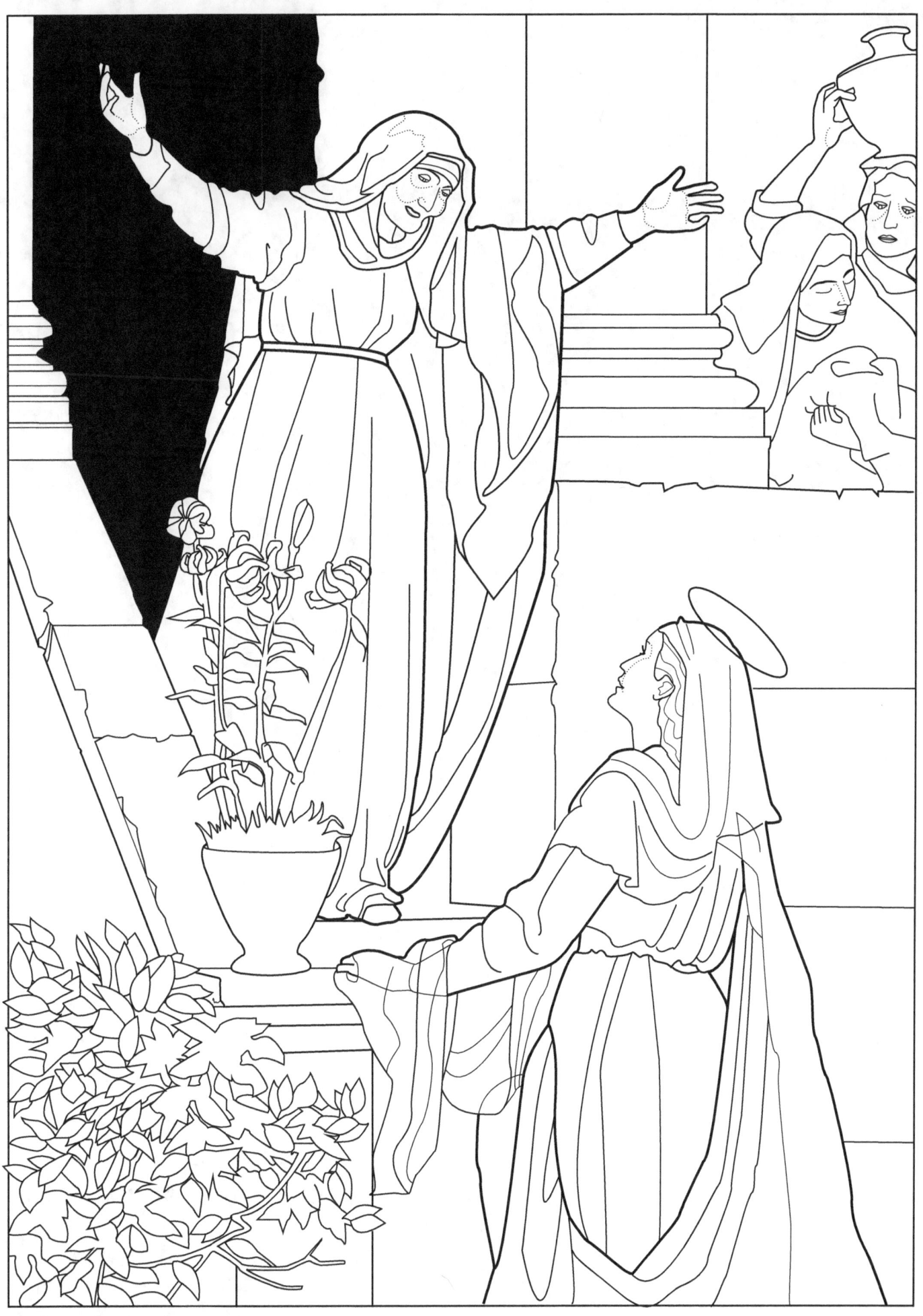

"Glory to God in the highest;
and on earth peace to men of good will."
[Luke 2:14]

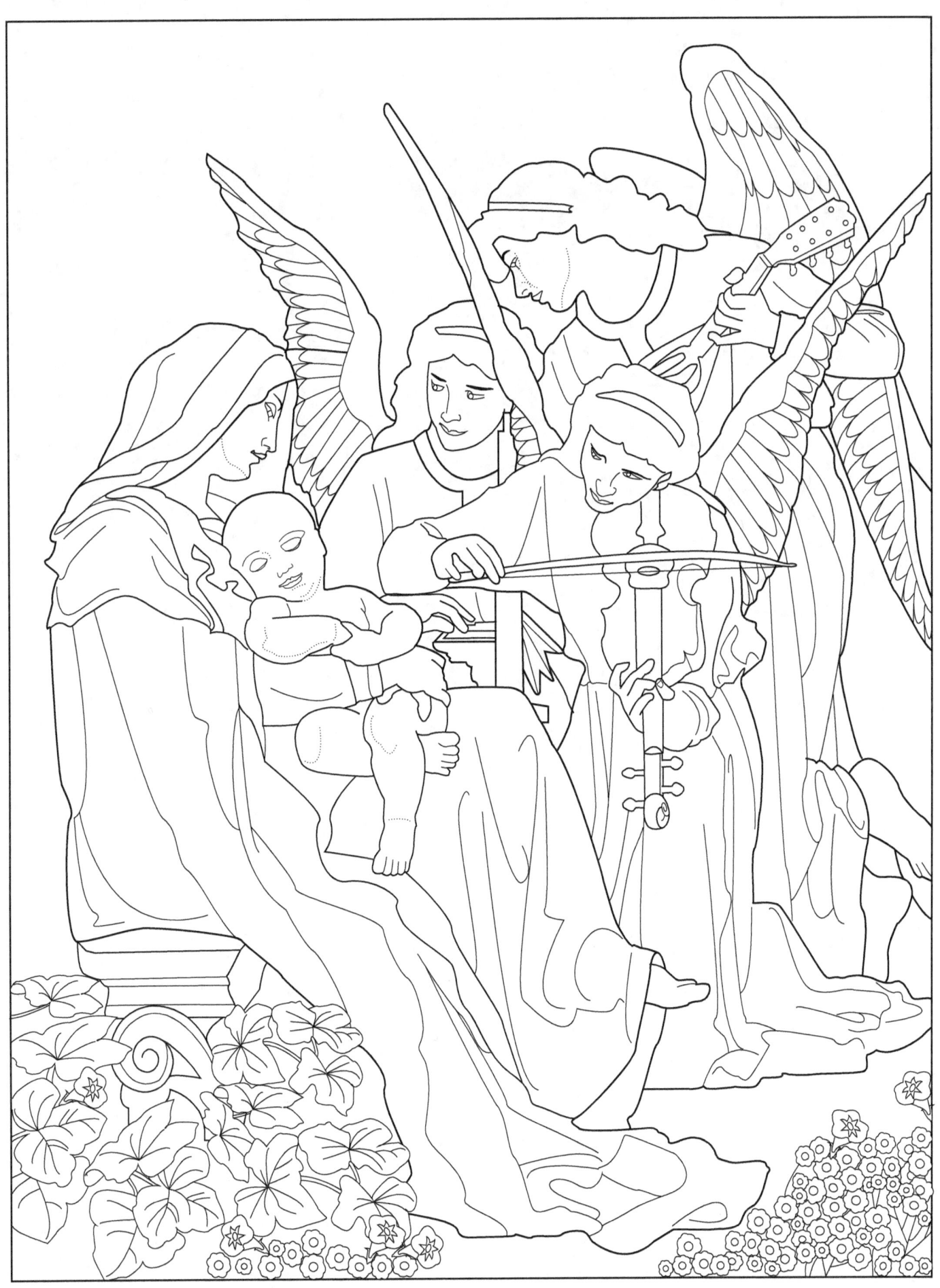

"[8] Again the devil took him up into a very high mountain, and shewed him all the kingdoms of the world, and the glory of them, [9] And said to him: All these will I give thee, if falling down thou wilt adore me. [10] Then Jesus saith to him: Begone, Satan: for it is written, The Lord thy God shalt thou adore, and him only shalt thou serve.
[Matthew 4:5]

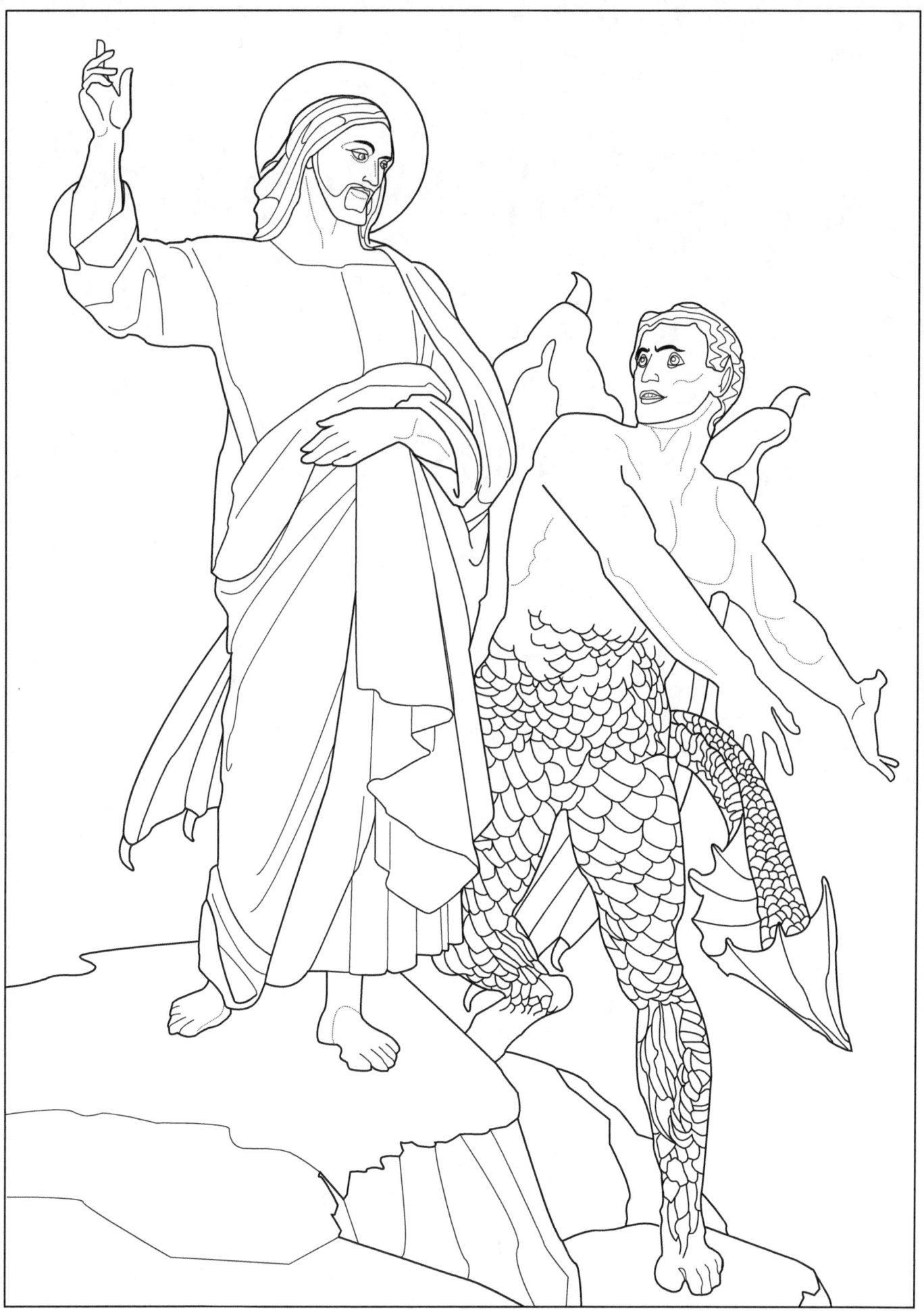

"He came again therefore into Cana of Galilee, where he made the water wine."
[John 4:46]

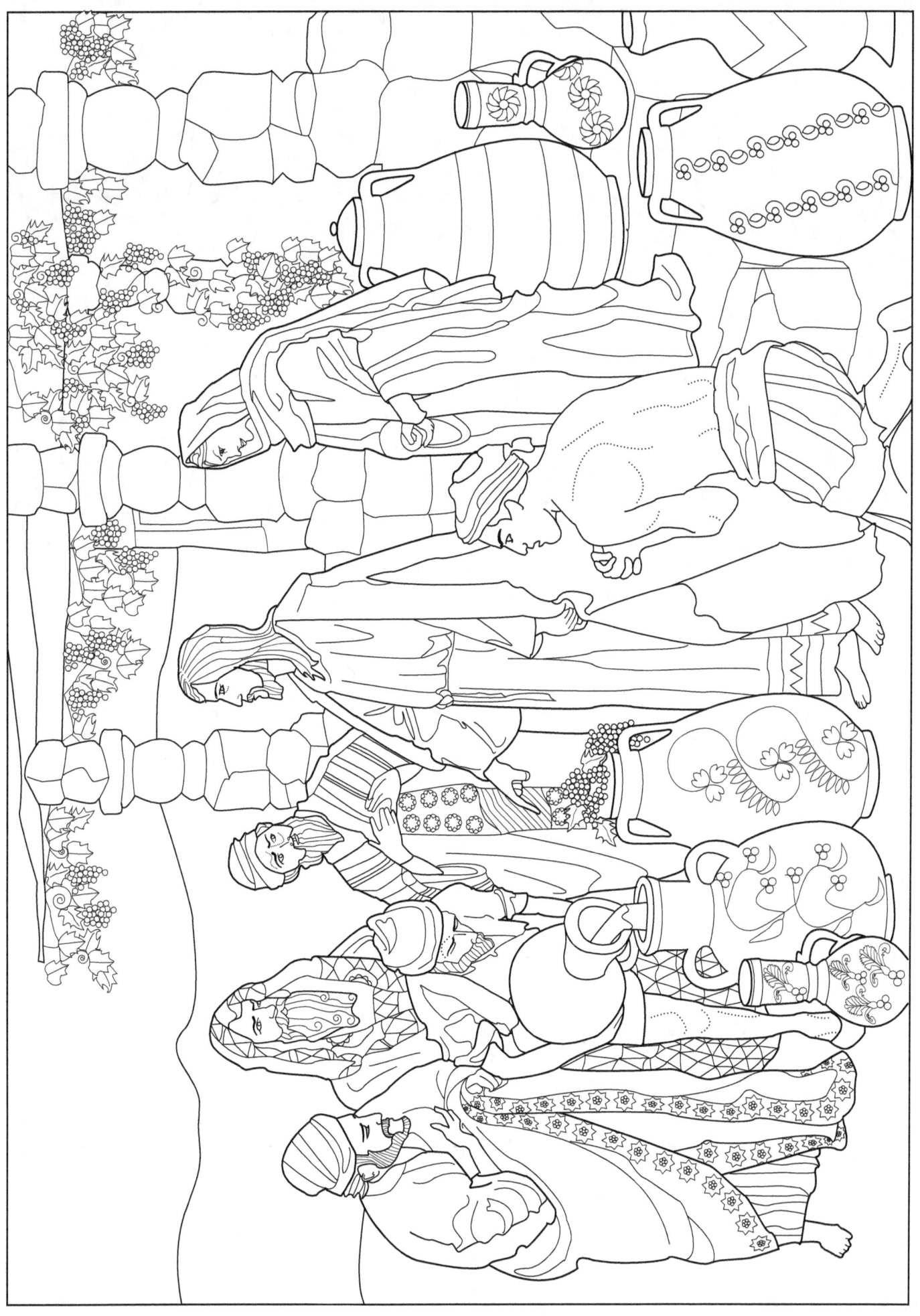

[9] For he was wholly astonished, and all that
were with him, at the draught of the fishes
which they had taken. [10] And so were also James and
John the sons of Zebedee, who were Simon's partners.
And Jesus saith to Simon: Fear not:
from henceforth thou shalt catch men. [Luke 5:9]

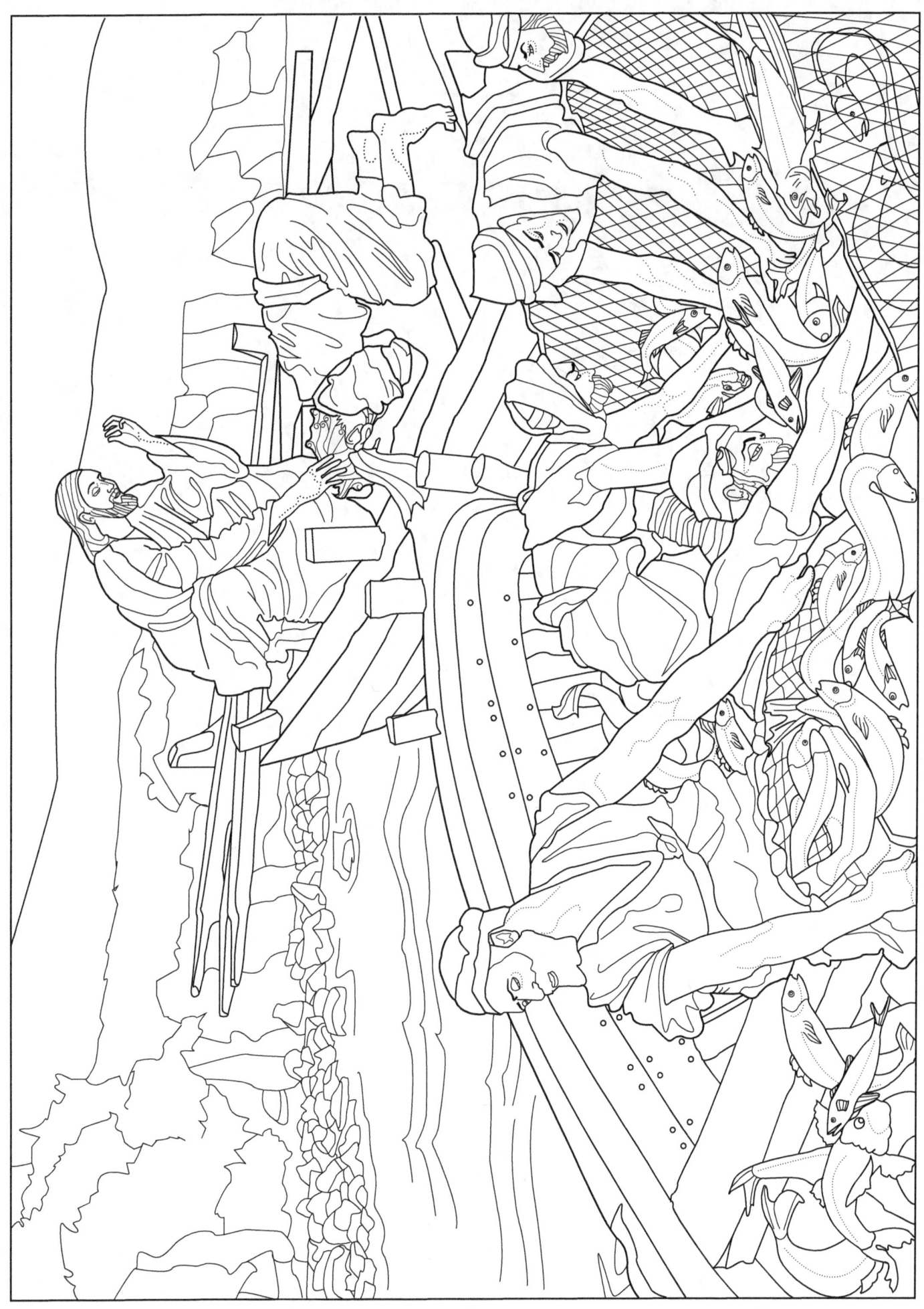

"And when Jesus had seen their faith,
he saith to the sick of the palsy:
Son, thy sins are forgiven thee."
[Mark 2:5]

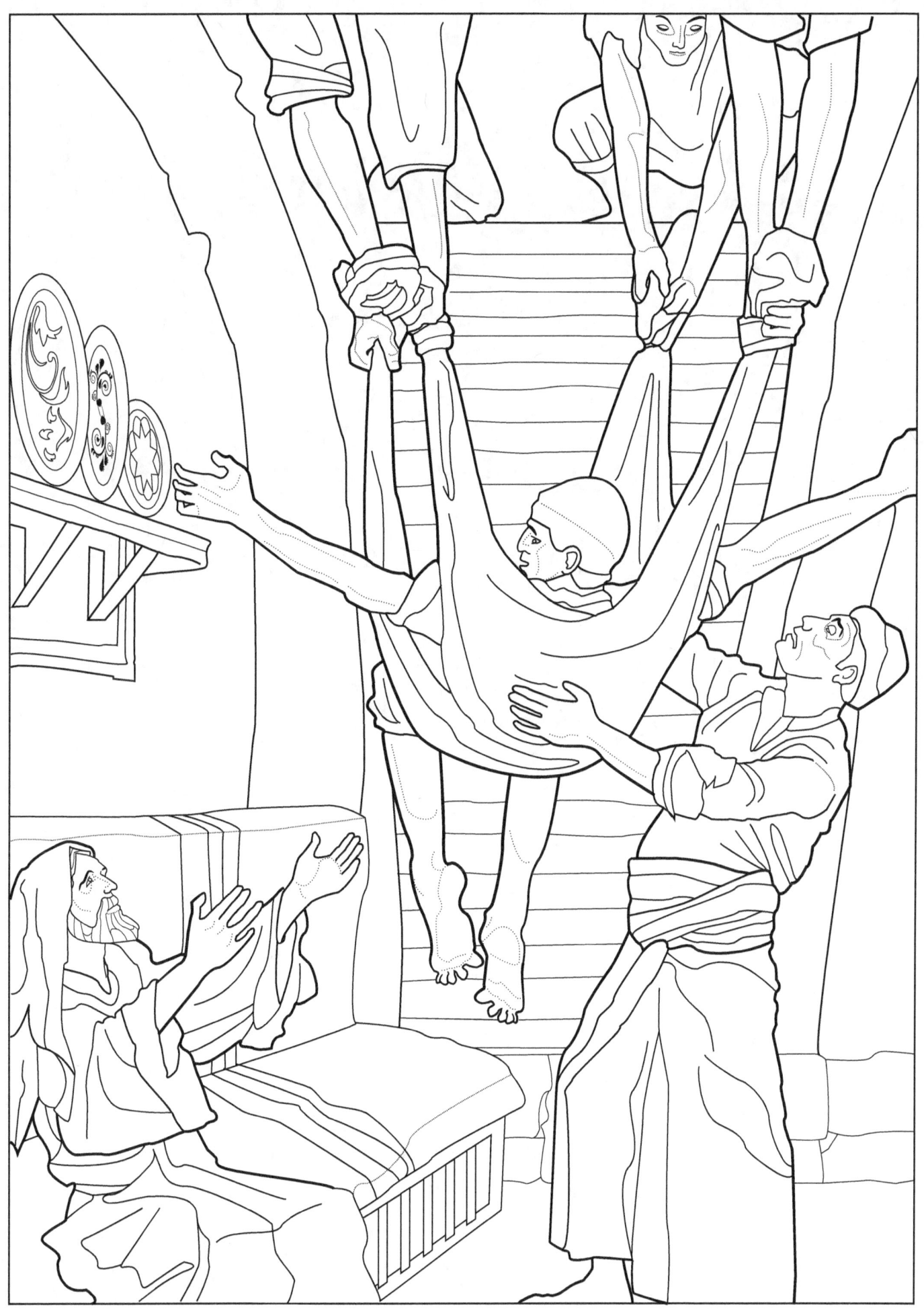

"And behold there came a man whose name was Jairus, and he was a ruler of the synagogue: and he fell down at the feet of Jesus, beseeching him that he would come into his house:"
[Luke 8:41]

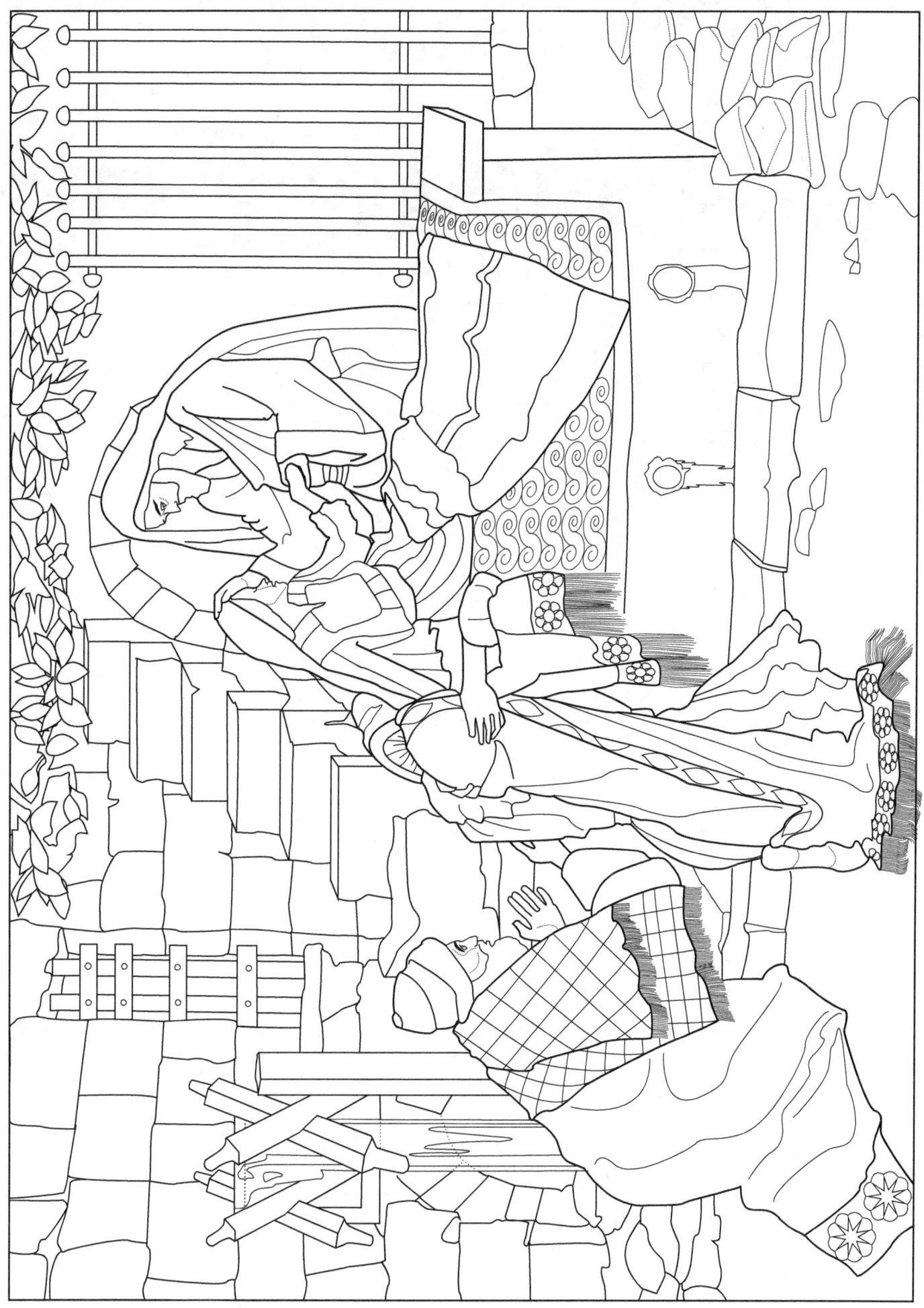

"And when he had commanded the multitudes to sit down upon the grass, he took the five loaves and the two fishes, and looking up to heaven, he blessed, and brake, and gave the loaves to his disciples,
and the disciples to the multitudes."
[Matthew 14:19]

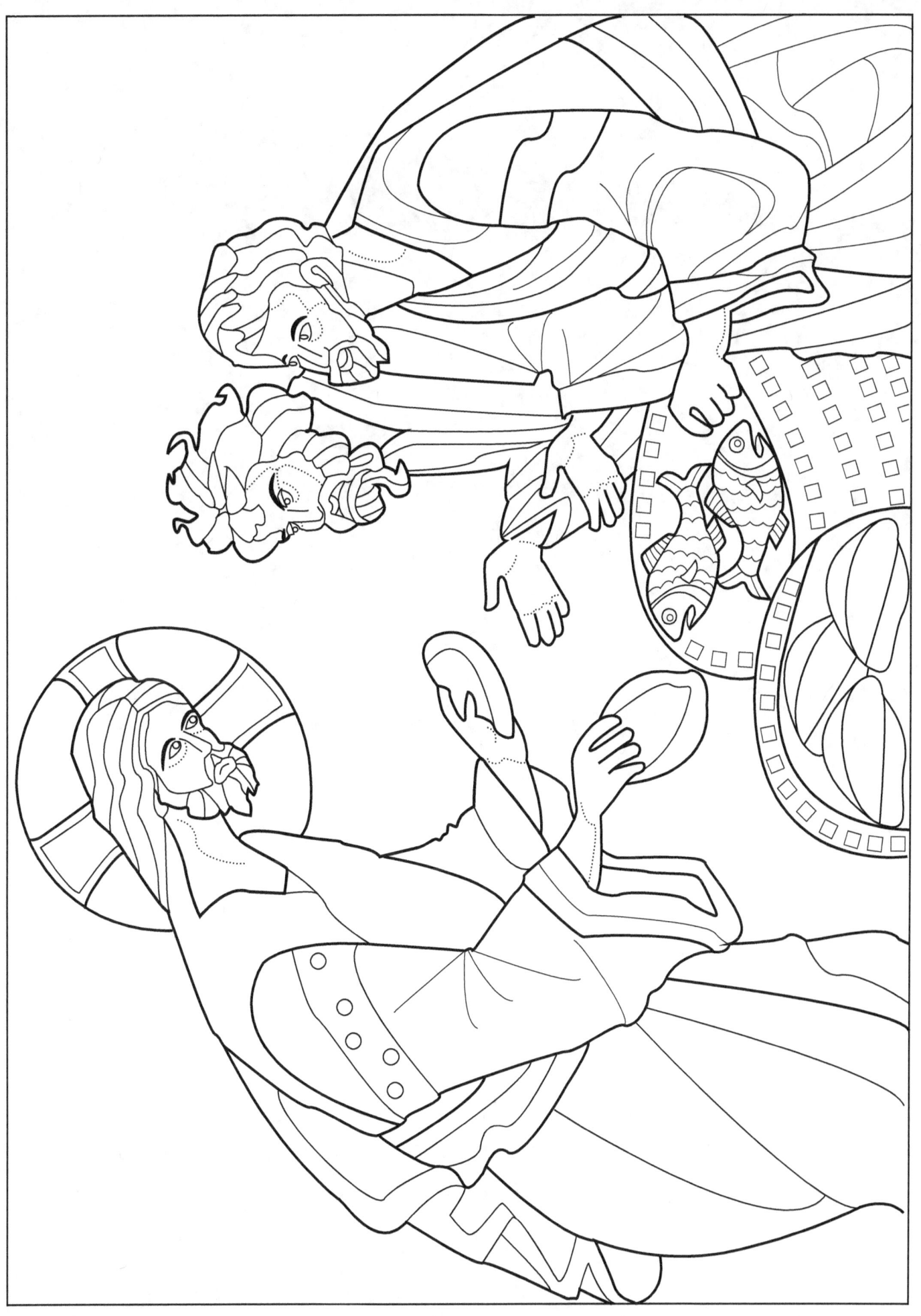

"And standing behind at his feet, she began to wash his feet,
with tears, and wiped them with the hairs of her head,
and kissed his feet, and anointed them with the ointment."
[Luke 7:38]

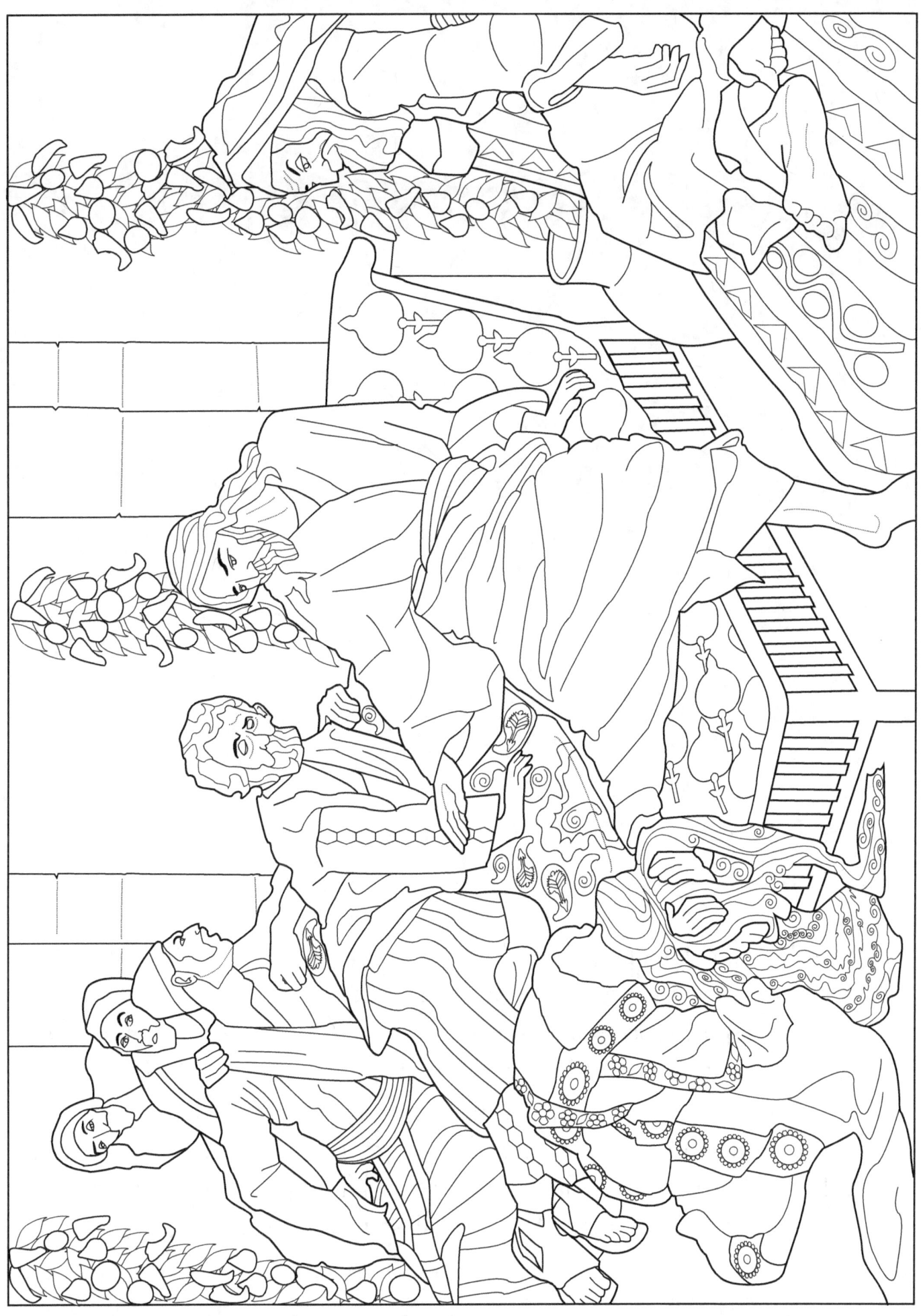

He spoke also this parable: A certain man had a fig tree planted in his vineyard, and he came seeking fruit on it, and found none. [7] And he said to the dresser of the vineyard: Behold, for these three years I come seeking fruit on this fig tree, and I find none. Cut it done therefore: why cumbereth it the ground?
[8] But he answering, said to him: Lord, let it alone this year also, until I dig about it, and dung it. [9] And if happily it bear fruit: but if not, then after that thou shalt cut it down. [Luke 13:6]

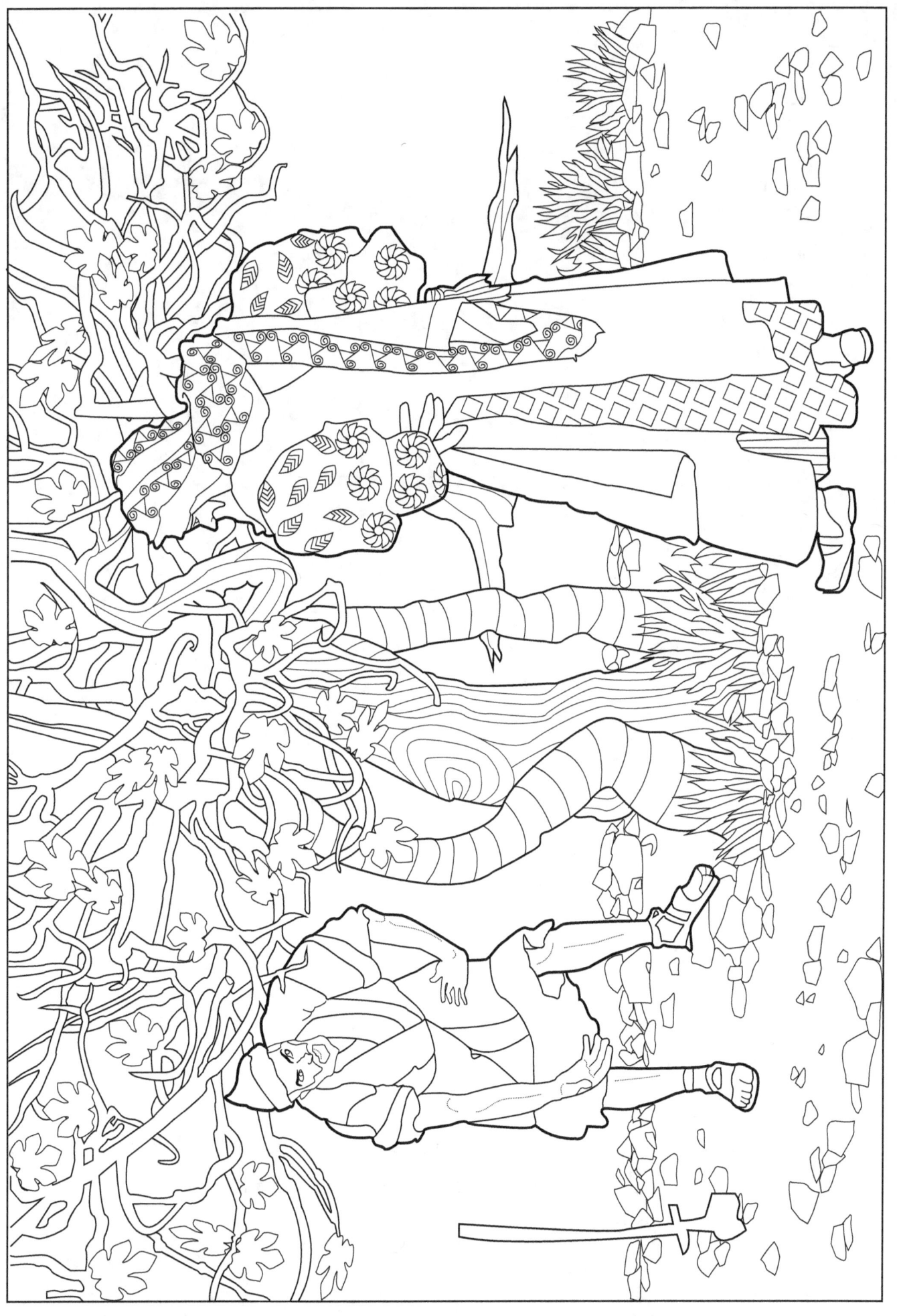

"And said: Amen I say to you,
unless you be converted, and become as little children,
you shall not enter into the kingdom of heaven."
[Matthew 18:3]

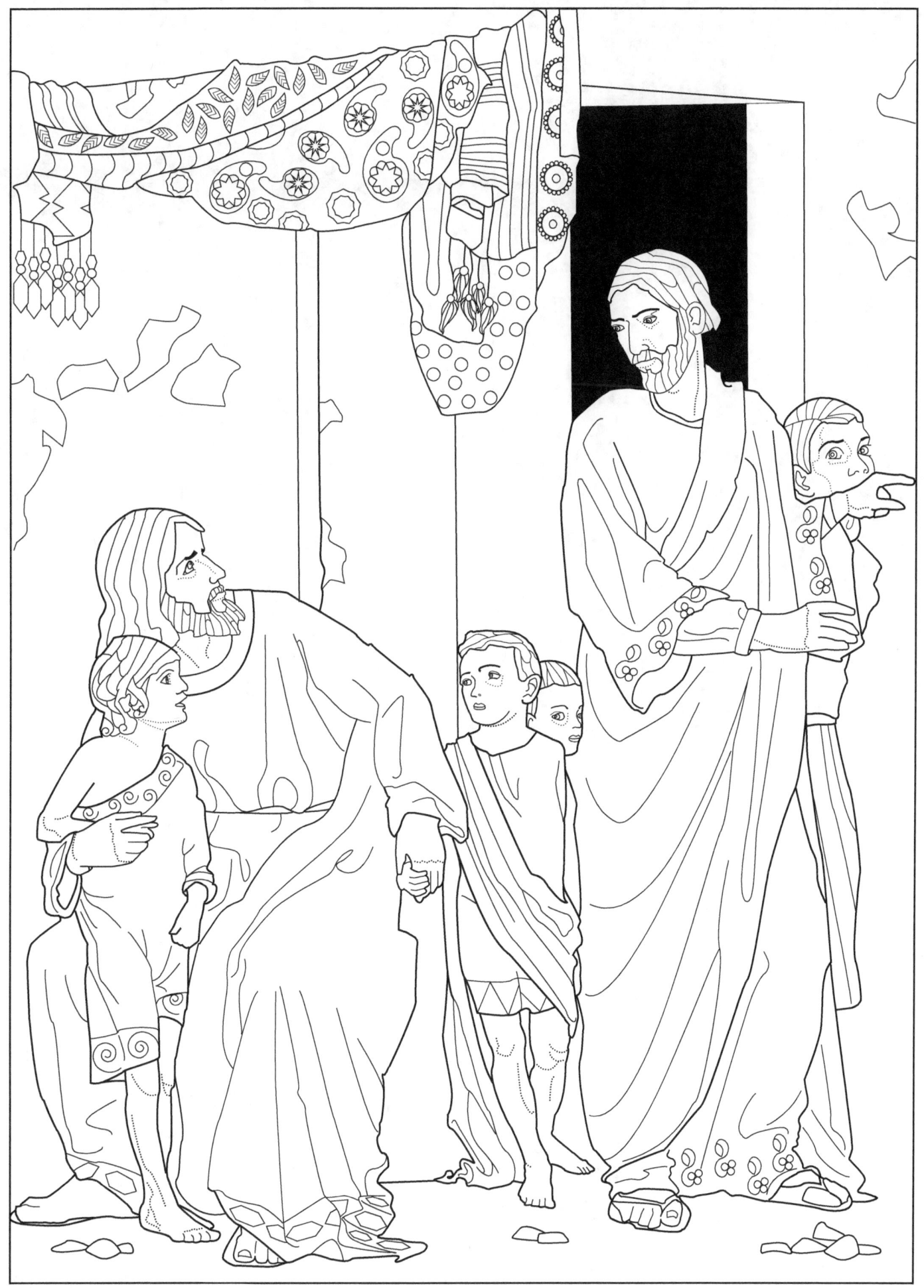

"And Jesus saith to them: Why are you fearful,
O ye of little faith? Then rising up
he commanded the winds, and the sea,
and there came a great calm."
[Matthew 8:26]

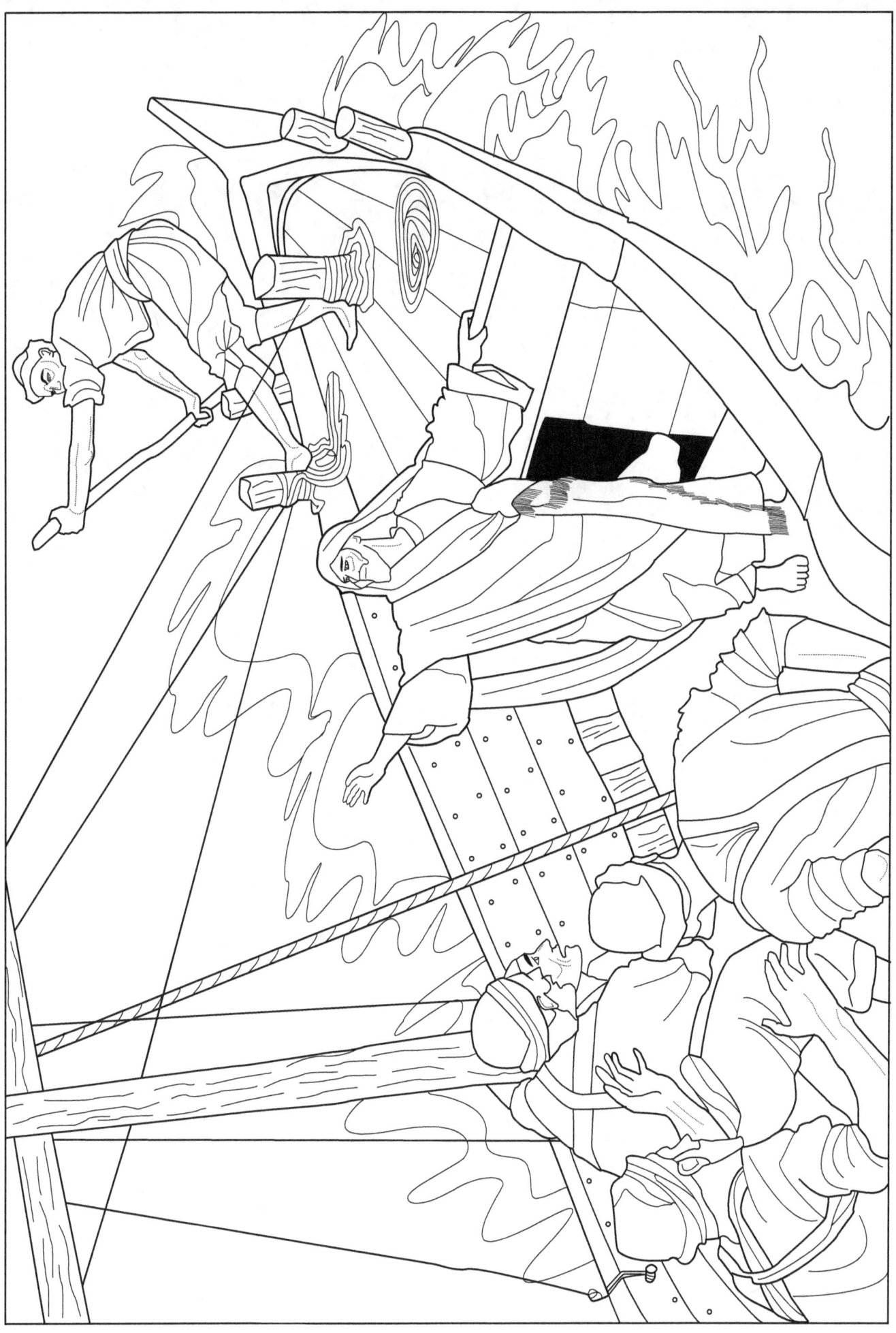

[1] And seeing the multitudes, he went up into a mountain,
and when he was set down, his disciples came unto him.
[2] And opening his mouth, he taught them,
[Matthew 5:1]

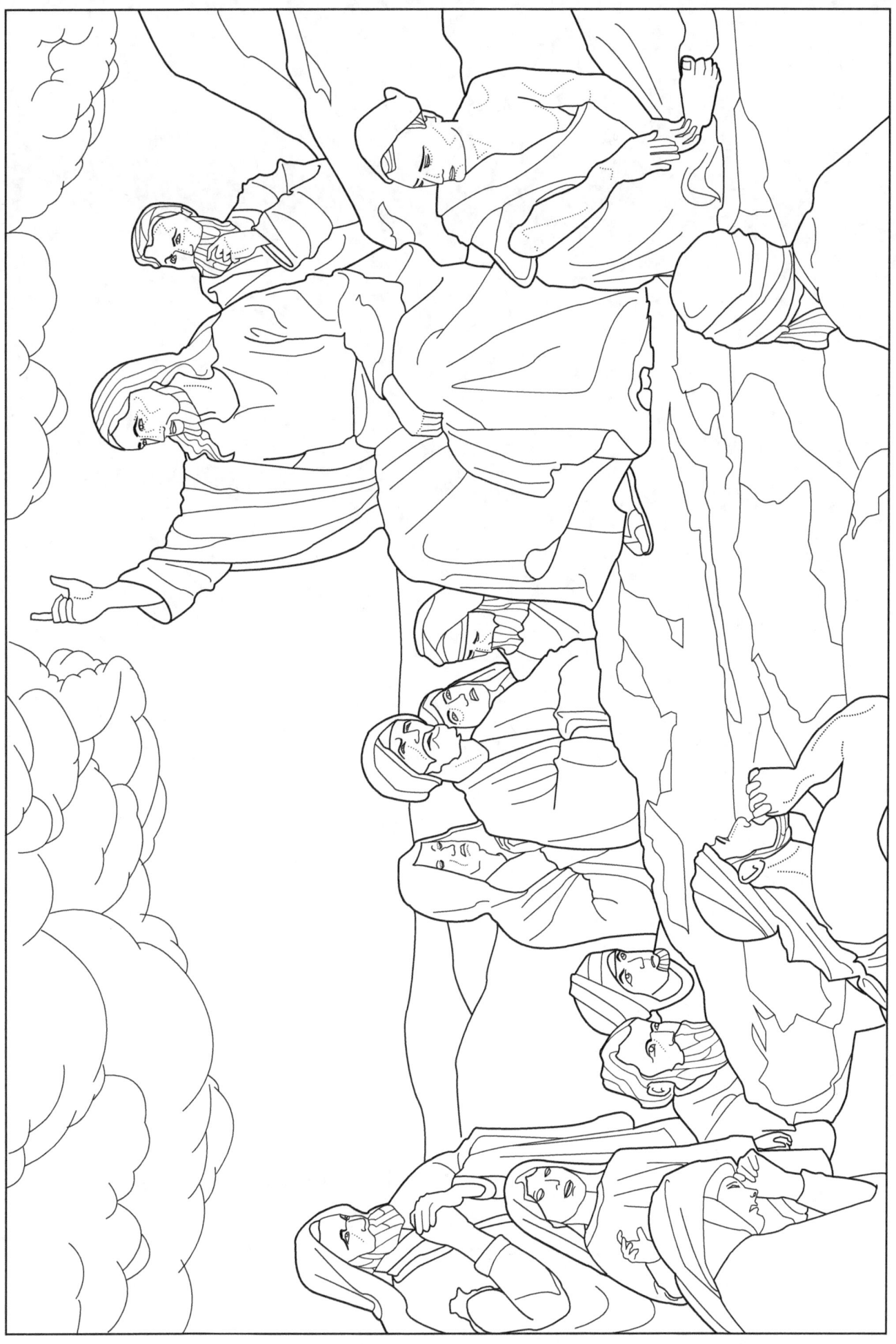

"I am the good shepherd; and I know mine,
and mine know me."
[John 10:14]

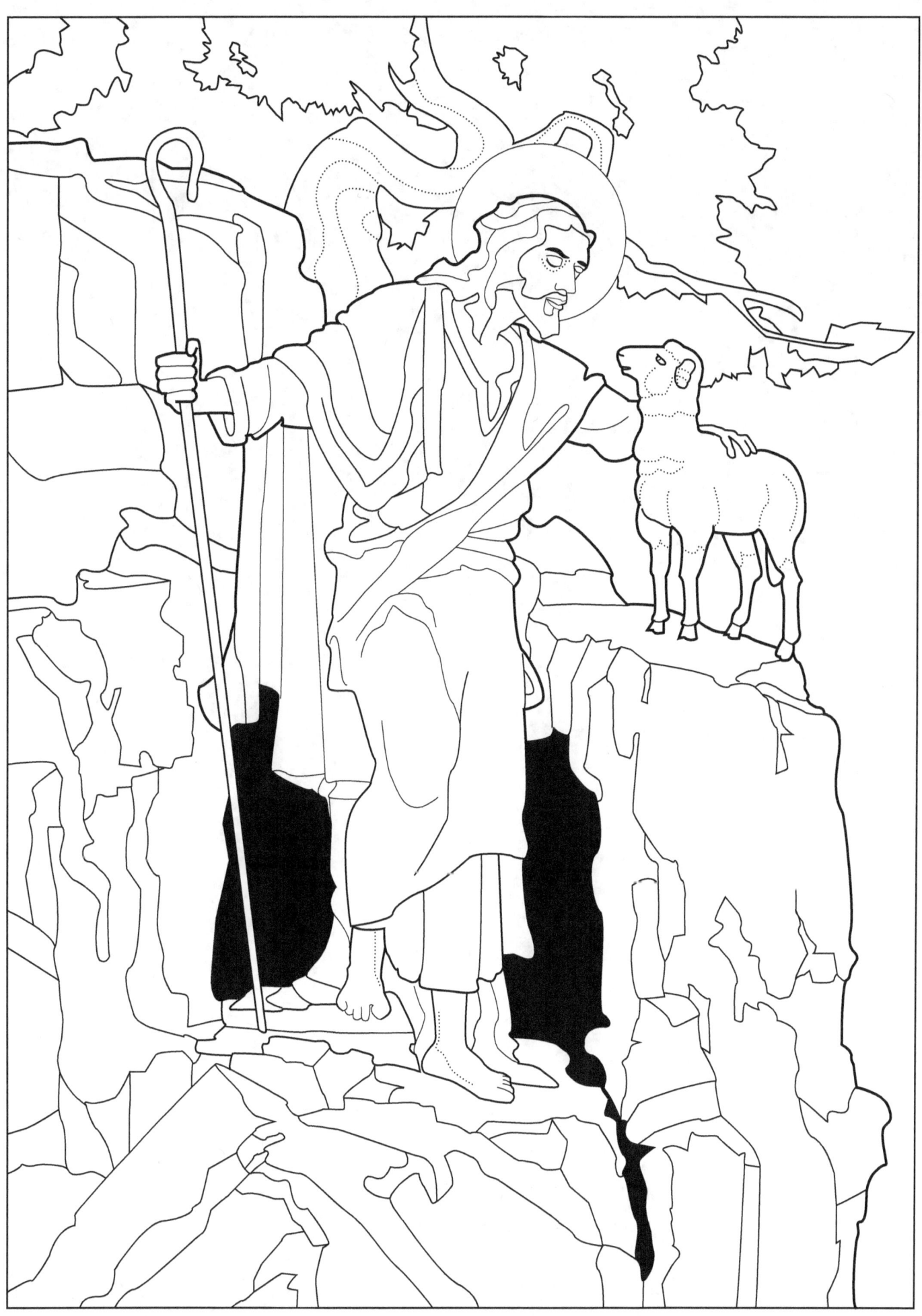

"But a certain Samaritan being on his journey,
came near him; and seeing him,
was moved with compassion."
[Luke 10:33]

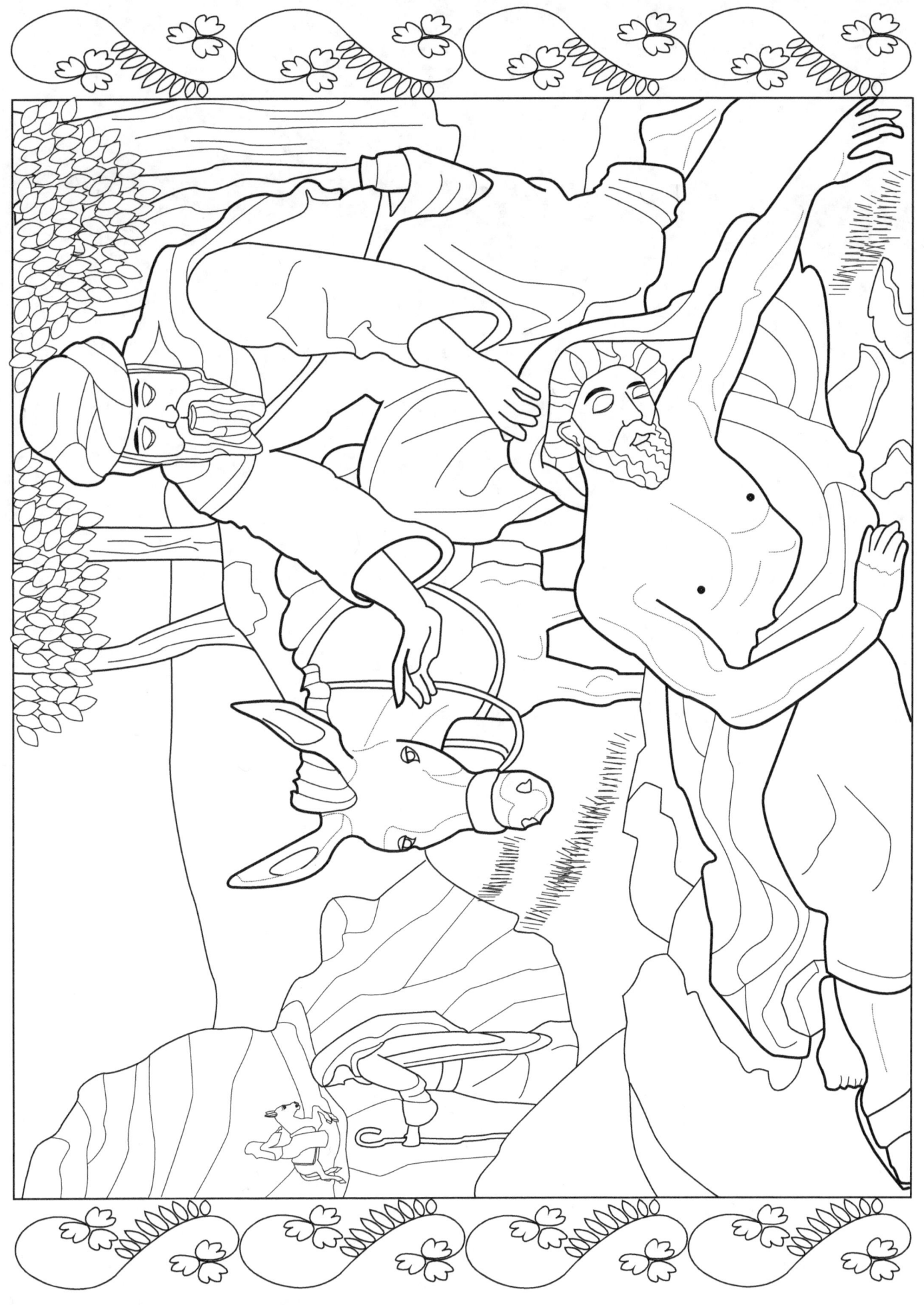

"And Jesus hearing it, said to them:
This sickness is not unto death, but for the glory of God:
that the Son of God may be glorified by it."
[John 11:4]

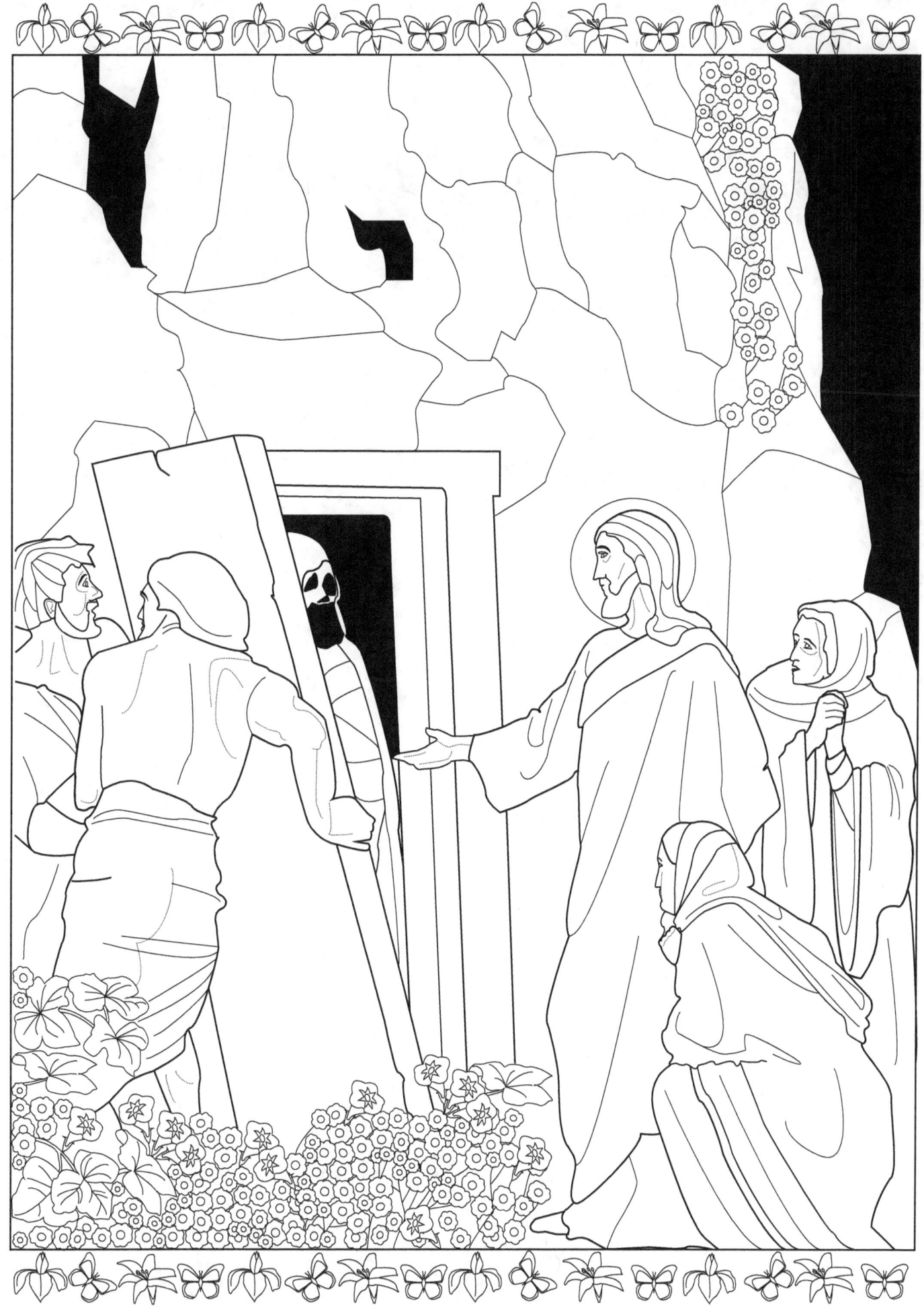

"And rising up he came to his father.
And when he was yet a great way off, his father saw him,
and was moved with compassion, and running to him
fell upon his neck, and kissed him."
[Luke 15:20]

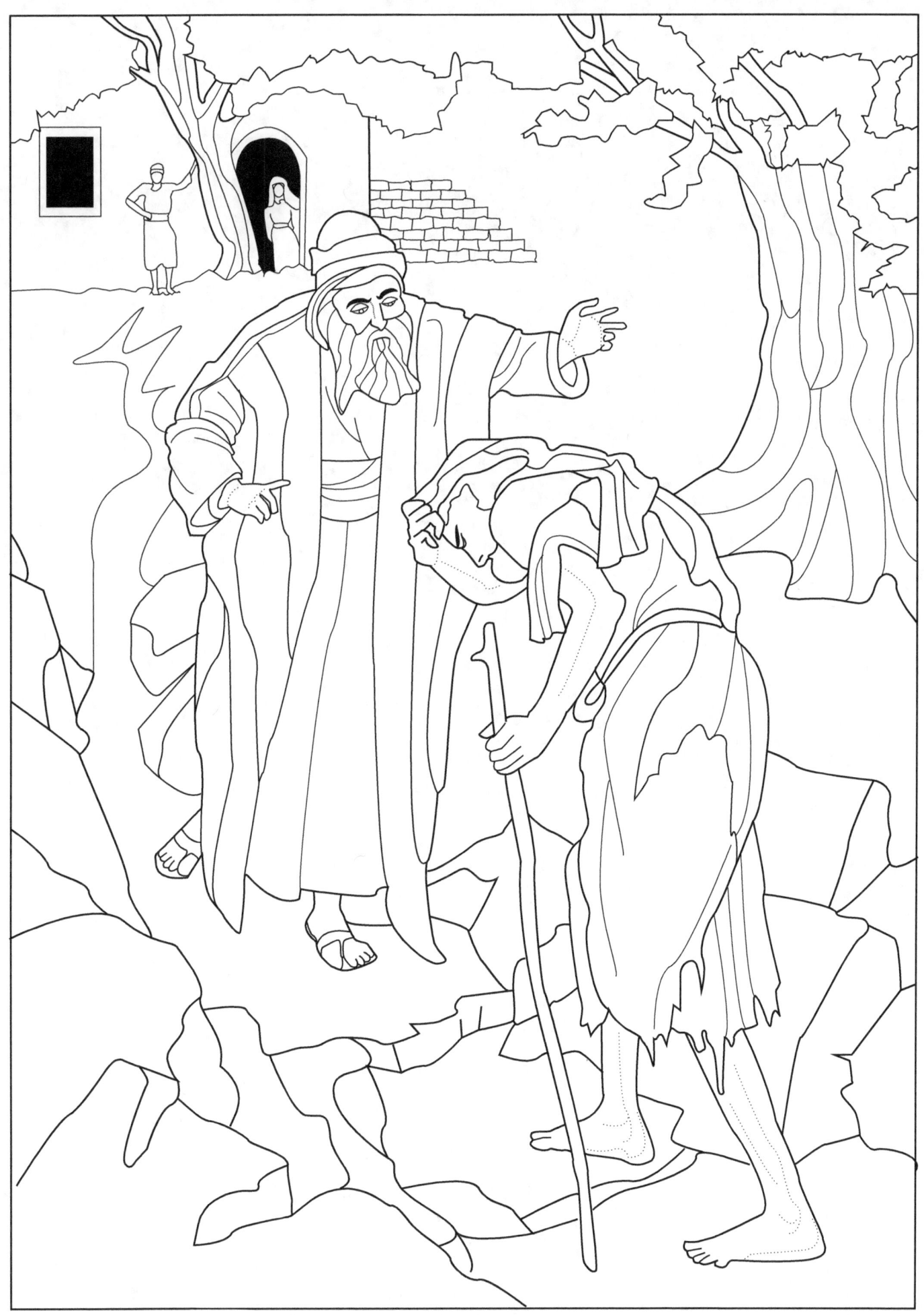

"The woman saith to him:
Sir, thou hast nothing wherein to draw,
and the well is deep;
from whence then hast thou living water?"
[John 4:11]

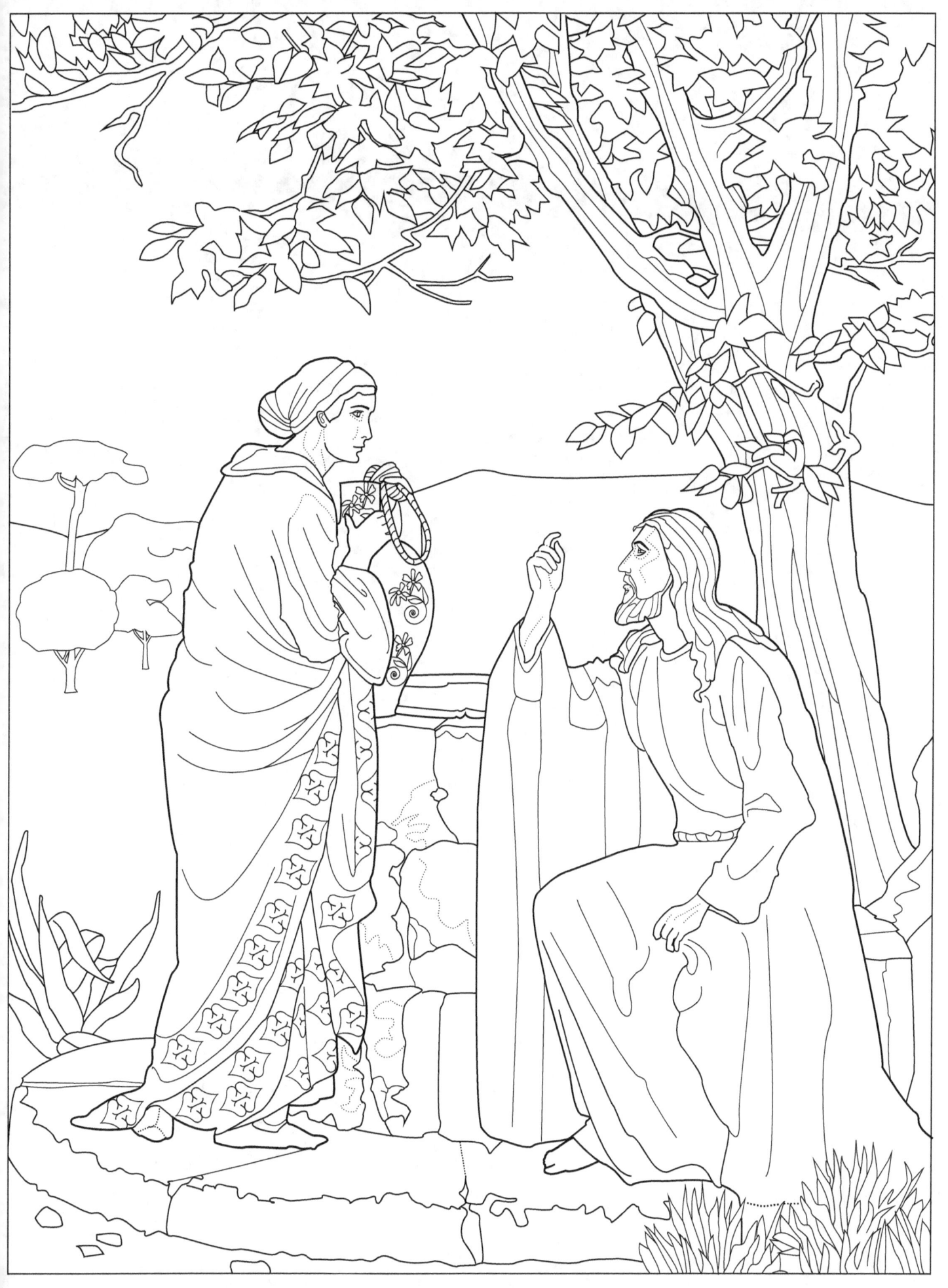

"Took branches of palm trees, and
went forth to meet him, and cried:
Hosanna, blessed is he that cometh
in the name of the Lord, the king of Israel."
[John 12:13]

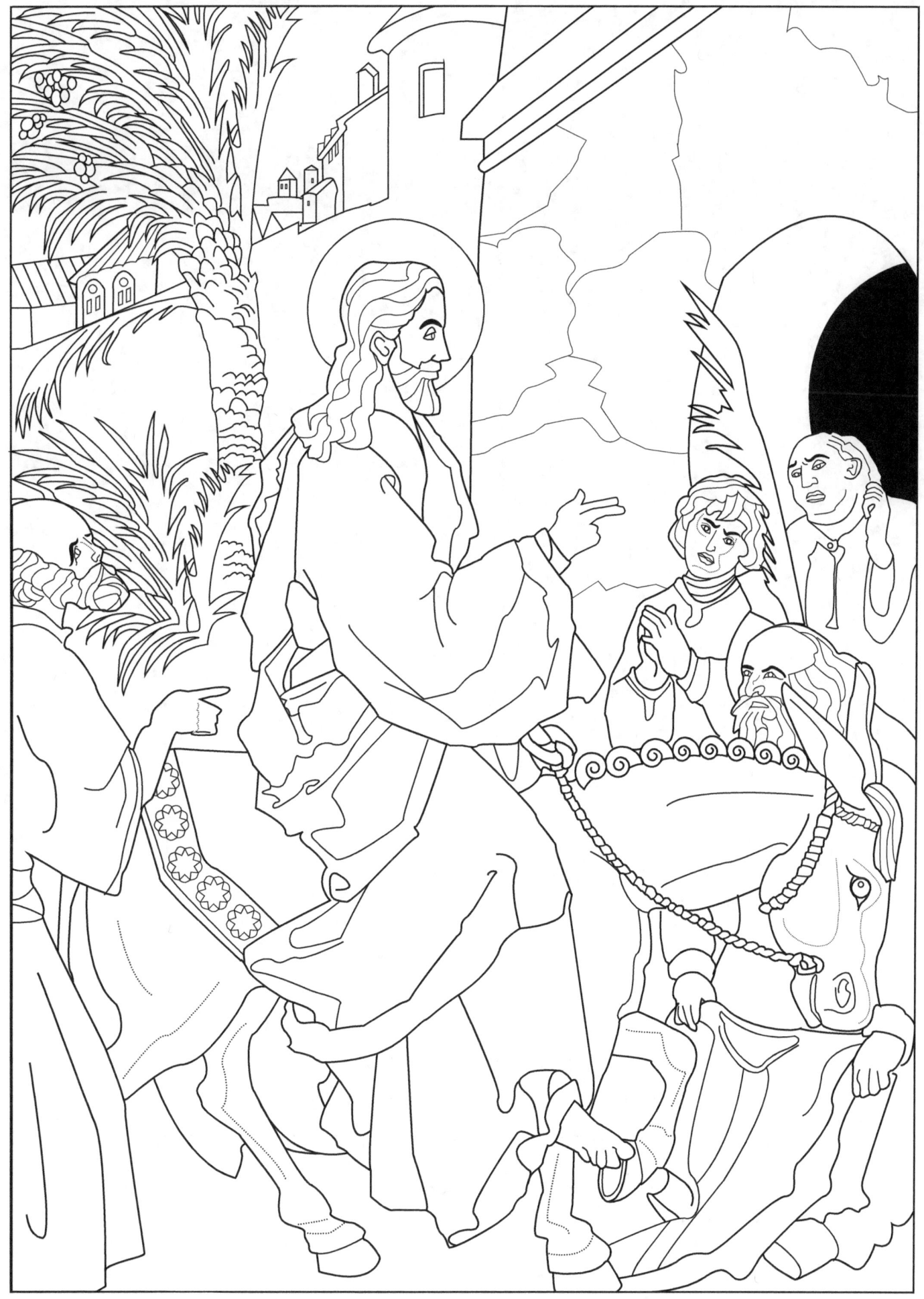

"And Jesus went into the temple of God,
and cast out all them that sold and bought in the temple,
and overthrew the tables of the money changers,
and the chairs of them that sold doves:"
[Matthew 21:12]

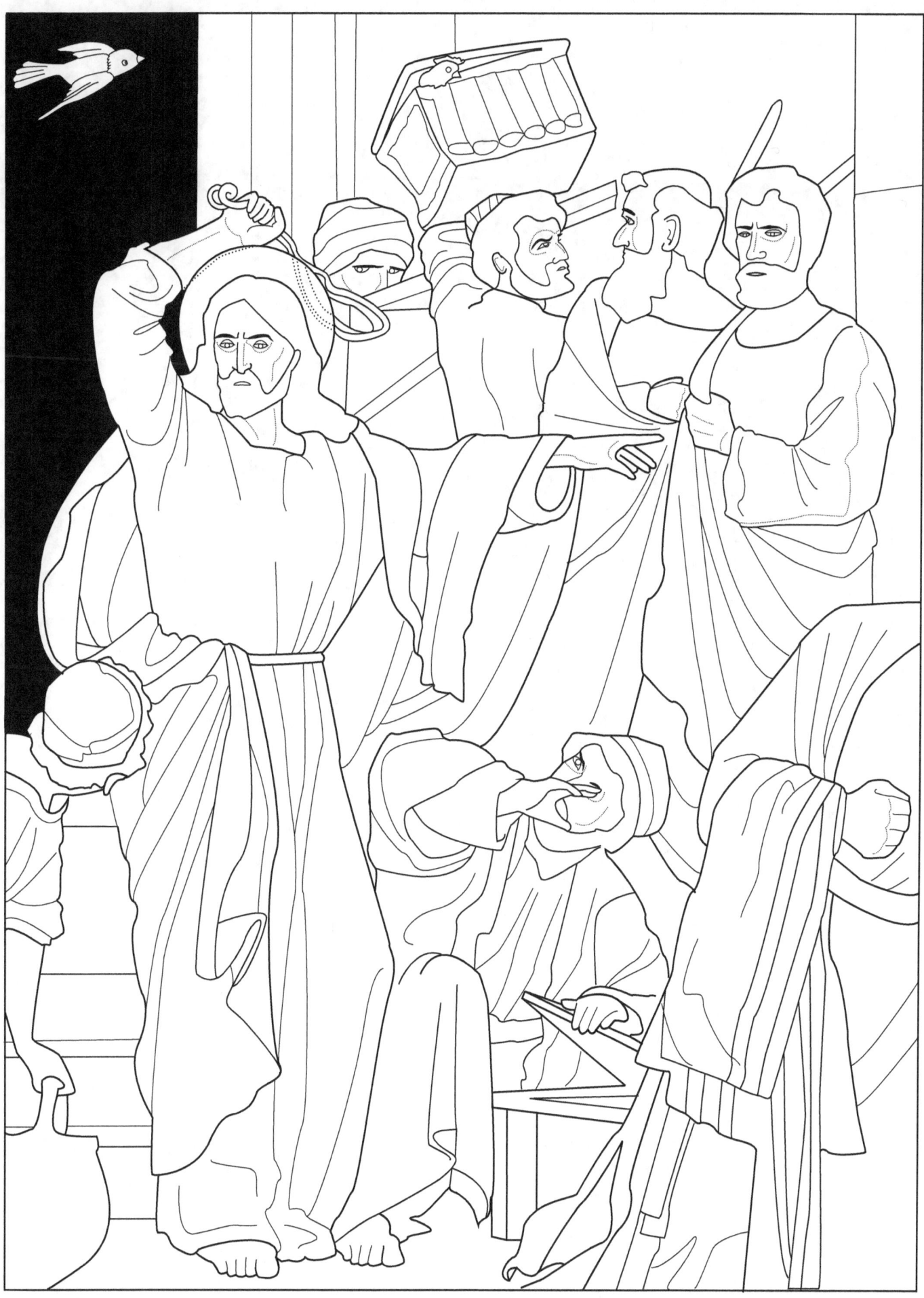

"And heal the sick that are therein, and say to them: The kingdom of God is come nigh unto you." [Luke 10:9]

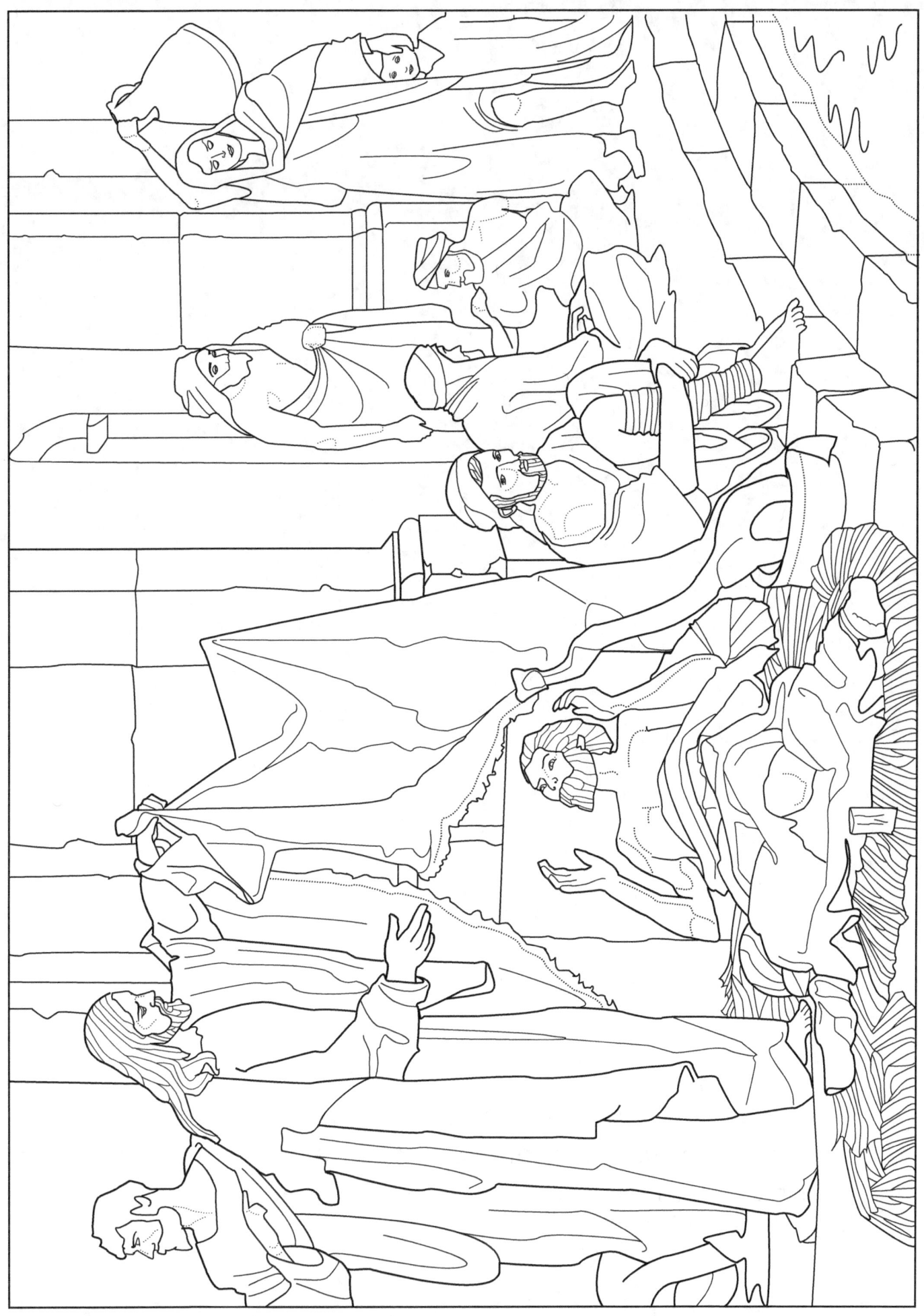

"And the centurion making answer, said:
Lord, I am not worthy that thou shouldst enter under my roof:
but only say the word, and my servant shall be healed."
[Matthew 8:8]

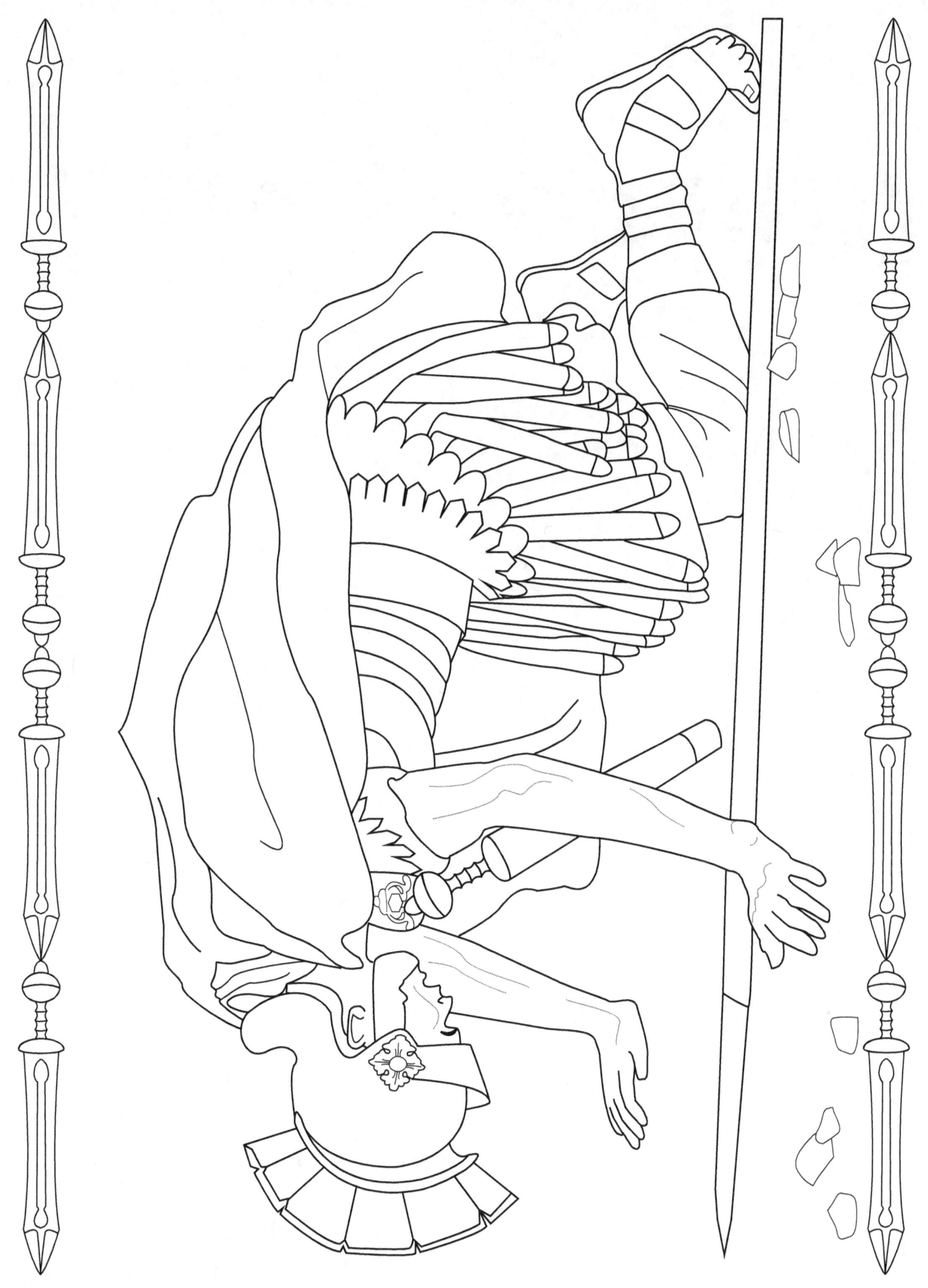

"If then I being your Lord and Master, have washed your feet; you also ought to wash one another's feet."
[John 13:14]

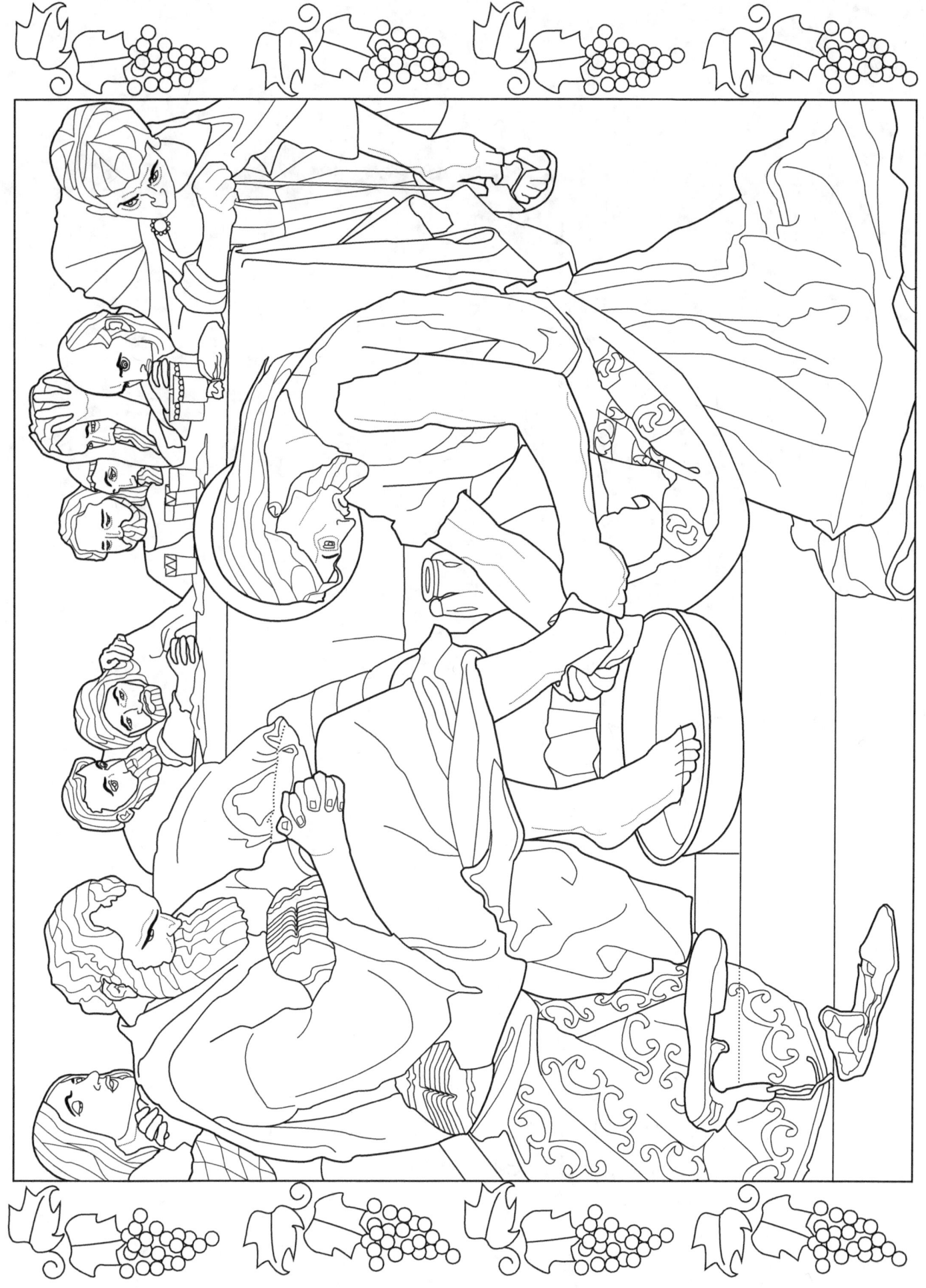

"And there appeared to him an angel from heaven, strengthening him. And being in an agony, he prayed the longer."
[Luke 22:43]

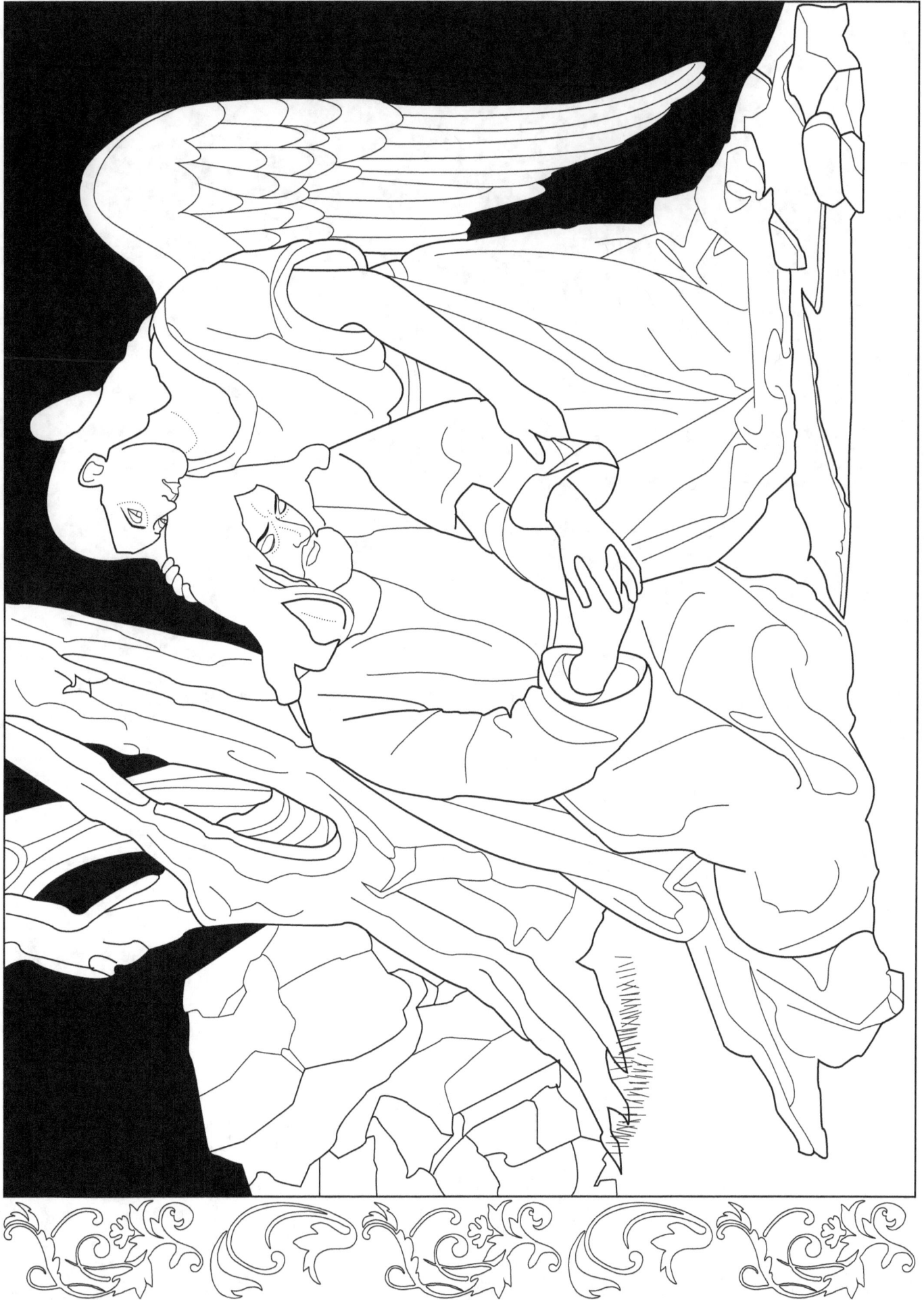

"Take up my yoke upon you, and learn of me,
because I am meek, and humble of heart:
and you shall find rest to your souls."
[Matthew 11:29]

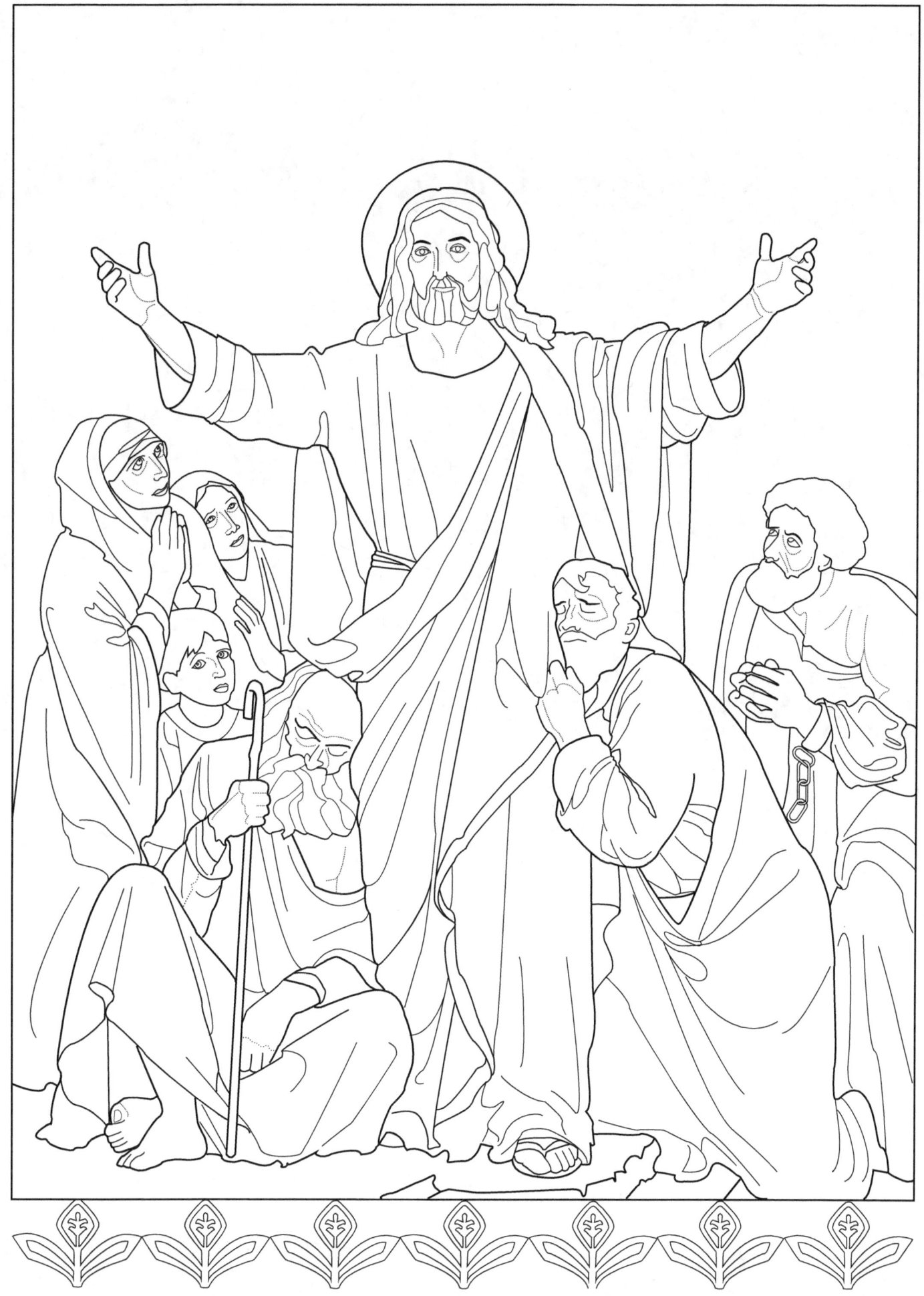